Caithness to Patagonia

Published by
Whittles Publishing Ltd.,
Dunbeath,
Caithness, KW6 6EG,
Scotland, UK
www.whittlespublishing.com

Kind thanks to the McPherson and Plowman
families for the use of their photographs.

ISBN 978-184995-173-9

Printed by 4edge Limited, UK

Caithness to Patagonia

DISTANT LANDS AND CLOSE RELATIVES

from a concept by
DONALD MACDONALD

Ian Leith

Whittles Publishing

Dedicated to Anya Catherine Hepburn:
The new generation

Contents

Acknowledgements

The topic of Caithness and Patagonia was first brought to public attention by the work done by Margie Sinclair for the BBC Odyssey radio programme. Her work was part of the stimulus to further explore the links between Caithness and Patagonia.

When Donald MacDonald and I first discussed this project, little did we know the extent of what we would find. Donald had researched some aspects of John Hamilton, but rapidly it became evident that Hamilton was far from alone in connecting Caithness with Patagonia. The subsequent research has involved much reading, archival searching, discovering descendants and, finally, a trip to Patagonia.

The numbers of people who have made this possible are many and while the following list can not do justice to the enthusiasm and help provided, I hope that a huge collective thank you to all who I have contacted along the way will at least be some form of recognition. There are of course some people without whom this work would not have been possible:

· **Donald MacDonald**, sheep farmer from Forss in Caithness, provided the initial impetus. He was a key identifier of descendants, and a loyal companion throughout.

· **Doreen Leith**, along with being a key member of the Patagonian Team, provided the emotional (and editing) support that kept me, and the project, on track.

· **Ali Hepburn** enthusiastically and diligently conducted archival research.

· **Catriona Metcalf**, senior reporter with the *John O'Groat Journal*, supported the project with a series of newspaper articles.

· **Alexandra Bowie** established important Patagonian links.

· **Helena and Freddie Altstadt** for their generous hospitality, and without whom the Patagonian trip would not have been possible.

· The pupils and staff of **Lybster Primary School**, plus **Moira Brown** and the pupils and staff of **Argentinas Malvinas School** in Fitzroy, Patagonia.

· Staff members at **Caithness Archive Centre**, **National Library of Scotland**, **National Archives of Scotland** and **Wick Library** for their willing help.

- **Pablo Beecher** for providing notes on his interviews.
- **John Pilkington** for sharing his interviews.
- The Caithness (and UK locations) descendants and friends who have all willingly shared family information and given their support to the project:

Peter Aikman; David Begg; Olive Booth; Audry Bowie; Denise Bremner; Elizabeth Buchan; Helen and John Budge; Alex Christian; Alistair Cleary; Muriel Craig; Anne Dunnett; Rae Gregory; John Gunn; Alistair Henderson; John O'Groats FC; Joanne Kaar; Andrew Leslie; Dawn McGregor; Benny and Jean MacKay; David and John MacKay; Greta and Norman MacKenzie; Kenneth McKenzie; John and James McKinnon; Tom and Linda Munro; William Munro; Peter and Rhona Nicol; Elizabeth Rintoul; Eann Sinclair and family; Annette Spencer and family; Ally Sutherland; Shirley Sutherland; Nancy Swanson; Sandra and Raymond Train; Bruce De Wert; Wick Academy FC; William Wilson.

- The Patagonia descendants and friends:

Brian Altstadt; Denise Altstadt; Alicia Bain; Bobby Bain; Caroline Bain; Gladys Bain; Monica Bain; Vanessa Bain; Margarita Barnetson; Club Deseado Juniors; Vivian Earsman; Winnie Fraser; Stephen Gallie; Ariel Hamilton; Daphne and Alejandro Jamieson; Mayo Hewlett; Isobel MacDonald; Angela McPherson; Diana McPherson; John and Palmenia Nicol; Michael O'Byrne; Claudia Perea; Eduardo Tribaya; Gem Urquhart; Mary Walker; Ray Willans.

Part I
To Journey Hopefully

Bleak, windswept territory, suitable for Scotsmen and sheep.[1]

A New Horizon

Patagonia is a long way from Caithness, both physically and mentally. Apart from the wide horizons common to both, there is literally a world of distance between the two. In the late 19th century, however, a number of Caithness people took on the challenge of Patagonia.

Caithness is flat but by no means barren. From the mid-1800s onwards the county became increasingly geographically, politically and economically linked to the rest of Britain. Undoubtedly times were hard for many families living there, especially if they were large in number. Sons and daughters were often through necessity required to make their own ways in the world. Their cramped homes and challenging financial conditions may have been key motivating factors in the decision to seek new horizons. In Patagonia they would initially find endless horizons – but also harsh weather and little if anything in the way of home comforts. Whatever their lifestyles at home in Caithness amounted to, what greeted them in Patagonia must have been well beyond their knowledge or imaginings.

No home; no tools or materials to build one; no roads, no neighbours; sometimes no sheep; no fences, dependent for their food on what they could shoot or catch.[2]

Were the drivers purely financial, or was there a desire to grasp an opportunity? The Scots in general are recognised as 'a notoriously migratory people',[3] so the Caithness Patagonian Pioneers may simply have followed this inbuilt natural sense of adventure.

---

1 Attributed to Sir David Kelly, British Ambassador.
2 *Life and Work*: the magazine of the Church of Scotland, 1925.
3 *The Census and Some of its Uses: outlining a plain philosophy of population, etc./* G. T. Bisset-Smith. Edinburgh, 1921.

The Story Begins Here...

In 1880 a young man from Wick in Caithness arrived in the Falkland Islands. Over the following 60 years, John Hamilton was to become a significant force in the development of sheep farming in Patagonia. Today his legacy lives on among the Patagonian sheep farms through his great-grandchildren, who continue to farm the lands he judicially bought and established. In Caithness, his legacy is recognised through his philanthropy; the formation of the Hamilton Trust enabled support and financial assistance to be given to farms and businesses throughout Caithness.

John Hamilton, however, was not the only Caithness man or woman to have played a part in the development of Patagonia as a major sheep-farming region.

The descendants of the Caithness Patagonian Pioneers are very aware of their Caithness Patagonian links. The families keep their memories alive with stories and mementoes. This work is intended to honour these pioneering men and women from Caithness, and to provide a picture of the lives and conditions they faced – and mastered – in the early days of sheep farming in Patagonia.

John Hamilton left Caithness to work in the Falkland Islands, where a significant British community already existed. The islands were largely owned by the Falkland Islands Company, as an English colony, although many of the immigrant population were indeed Scots. After five years in the Falkland Islands, John Hamilton was among a number of men persuaded to set up in Patagonia. So began the story of the Caithness connection with a windy, lonely and faraway region as far south on the globe as Caithness is north. John Hamilton became one of the region's most successful sheep farmers and businessmen, and was instrumental in attracting other Caithness Pioneers to Patagonia.

John Hamilton placed advertisements in the Caithness newspaper the *John O'Groat Journal*, offering work as shepherds on his farms in Patagonia. The first four Caithness men to respond to the advertisement and leave for Patagonia were brothers David and Donald Christian from Newton, Wick; John MacKinnon from Shielton, Watten; and William Begg from Dunn, Watten.

What these four men expected to find on arrival in Patagonia is anyone's guess. John MacKinnon and William Begg were from farming/shepherding families and would at least have known how to handle sheep. The Christian brothers were from the crofting tradition – but none of the four, even by Caithness standards, could have expected to find the vast flat windswept lands of Patagonia. With regard to sheep, they certainly would not have been accustomed to herding flocks numbering thousands.

William Bain from Mavesy, near Lybster in Caithness, was the first of seven members of his family to settle in Patagonia. William left Caithness with John MacLeod, a close neighbour, from Clyth in the late 19th century. They too sailed initially via the Falklands, where John MacLeod may have remained for a time. William Bain continued to the port of Punta Arenas in southern Chile – the main seaboard gateway to Patagonia. He was either lucky or astute enough to make contact with Mauricio Braun, one of Patagonia's sheep farming entrepreneurs. William Bain was certainly able to prove himself, and became Braun's manager at Estancia Josefina. Some years later William Bain purchased the estancia, and today the farm continues to be owned and run by his descendants.

Robert Nicolson, also from Clyth, is reputed to have slept under a tree for some months while he cut his shepherding teeth on the vast Patagonian lands. The brothers Hugh and Angus MacPherson left their family farm at Halsary near Halkirk, to make a life in Patagonia. They were employed initially in the area known as Última Esperanza (Last Hope), again part of the vast Braun 'empire'. There can be little doubt that the conditions they found, and had to endure, were challenging. Angus MacPherson was a diary writer, filling some nine volumes with his experiences and thoughts. Today the diaries remain in the possession of his granddaughters, and contain some heart-wrenching accounts of the loneliness of life in the early days of Patagonia. The entries and the drawings reflect a mix of desolation and hopeful aspiration. Yet, in the long term, Angus overcame his desolation and achieved many of his ambitions. Hugh McPherson on the other hand eventually returned to, and settled in, Scotland.

The remoteness of Patagonia proved too much for some. One Scotsman claimed that its impact contributed to him killing an Inverness-shire policeman.

Around 1886 Allan McCallum had left home to become a Patagonian shepherd. He was later to claim that the harsh South American weather conditions were the cause of an illness that was to change his mental state; long periods in the wide-open Patagonian lands had inflicted sunstroke. This claim was made as part of his defence when he was charged with the murder of Constable King, near Nethy Bridge, and on 14 February 1899 he appeared in the High Court of Justiciary in Inverness. There, however, McCallum was found guilty of culpable homicide by a majority verdict, and sentenced to 15 years' imprisonment.[1]

But a significant number of the Caithness Pioneers – men and women both – took Patagonia by the scruff of the neck, and made it their home.

By and large the women went as wives. While the challenges faced by the shepherds were both physical and mental, the late 19th and early 20th-century Patagonian lifestyles that the women had to adopt and adapt to are almost unimaginable from our 21st-century viewpoint

Adventure, hardship, determination and some significant success stories surrounds the experience of the Caithness Patagonians, but still a question remains as to why Patagonia? Gold had been found in Tierra del Fuego in the 1880s, and given the history of gold rushes it is possible to envisage a spate of departures drawn by the lure of endless riches. The gold however was somewhat illusory and had reached its peak around 1893, therefore it played no part in the Caithness emigration to Patagonia. By and large, the goal of the Caithness Patagonian Pioneers was sheep farming.

This work aims to dust off the cobwebs surrounding these adventurers, while at the same time shining a light into the minds and the visions that brought them to these new horizons: 'Anyone whose parents, grandparents or great grandparents suffered as those pioneers did will carry Patagonia in their blood.'[2]

---

1 Patagonia: a life changing experience/Ian Leith and Ali Hepburn in *Scottish Memories*. May/June 2014.
2 *An Englishman in Patagonia*/ John Pilkington.1991.

A Land Far, Far Away

Jorge Luis Borges wrote: '[Y]ou will find nothing in Patagonia. There is nothing there.'

The population of Patagonia was, and remains, few in number. Argentina is a vast country in terms of its landmass, with Patagonia making up somewhere in the region of one third. Argentina also has a huge population (around 42 million). Patagonia's population is one tenth of that figure.

Patagonia is a vast tract of largely open landscape, with little between the ground and the sky. For generations an indigenous people lived mainly off the land and the various exotic animals that populated Patagonia. Europeans had visited on various occasions to explore and consider the potential of adding it to their empires. Portuguese and Spanish expeditions sought to infiltrate, and to navigate into, and through, the South American continent. Early in the 16th century an expedition arrived at the mouth of the River Plate, believing that the river ran all the way across the continent.

Magellan, the ultimate successful discoverer of the route between the Atlantic and the Pacific, also began his search at the mouth of the River Plate, but instead decided to head south. By way of Puerto Deseado, the regular stopping-off point for exploration ships coming across the Atlantic from Europe, Magellan proceeded on to San Julián, where he could safely pass the winter. Alas, his crew mutinied. Magellan's cool and calculated response was to have the ringleaders killed and a troublesome priest despatched onto a nearby island. Today a replica of Magellan's ship provides visitors to San Julián with a close look at the life and times of these early Patagonian explorers. Had our Caithness Patagonian Pioneers read or heard about Magellan and the other explorers? Were these explorers on the 19th-century Scottish school curriculum?-

Patagonia's inhospitable climate, an often hostile native population, plus difficult access to life-sustaining resources, meant that few of these early explorers felt a desire to linger. However, as a consequence of the many ships wrecked around the Patagonian shores, some survivors were forced into making an attempt at survival. Most failed.

The mystique of Patagonia was embellished by each visitor as they sought a reason for their failure to conquer. Giants, cities of gold, wild tribes and ferocious beasts were all wrongly attributed to Patagonia. The giant theory seems to have originated during Magellan's first voyage. One of his crew, Antonio Pigafetta, an Italian, wrote an account of their first encounter with the native inhabitants of Patagonia:

one day a man of gigantic height suddenly appeared on the beach ... Magellan arranged for a man to go ashore and ordered him to copy the movements of the savage as a sign of peace. He understood that we were not hostile and let himself be taken to a neighbouring island where our captain was waiting with several men. The savage was amazed to see them and by pointing upwards he appeared to be saying that he thought we came from heaven. This man was so tall that our heads just came up to his waist, he being in all respects very well proportioned.[1]

From then on the people were called Patagones, referring to their large feet. The large moccasins the native people wore helped exaggerate the size. The reality is that many of the Patagones were tall and muscular, confirmed from the measurements of one native in Tierra del Fuego: 'height was 5×8, chest 40, arm above elbow 14, calf of leg 14'.[2]

Attempts to explore the interior of Patagonia also met with fairly disastrous results. The harsh landscape, inhospitable climate, lack of food and water, and an unpredictable native population all helped give the place a bad name. Charles Darwin was among the few who gave Patagonia due respect, as he detailed the unique animals and their habitats. Darwin was, however, less kind in his thoughts and comments about the native population and maybe as a result of that many Europeans continued to consider Patagonia, as a wild place or indeed an imaginary one. Yet Darwin had also claimed that his 'eureka' moment had come in Patagonia, and certainly the consequences of his Patagonian trip changed thinking across the world. Another eureka moment preceded Darwin by several hundred years, when Francis Drake had inadvertently discovered that Tierra del Fuego was an island off the South American continent and not part of the Antarctic landmass.

Leading up to Darwin's visit, the ship *Beagle* had been engaged in charting the coasts of Patagonia. It was during this exercise that Captain Fitzroy captured three Fuegian natives and brought them back to England, with the aim of educating them and instilling into them a 'civilised' culture. To various degrees this experiment was at first successful. However, when the Fuegians returned to their native lands, to all intents they reverted to their own customs.

Geographically Patagonia is shared between Argentina and Chile. Stretching some 1,000 miles from its northern boundary with the Argentinian pampas to the southernmost, near-Antarctic, tip of Tierra del Fuego, it is a vast landmass. To the east its shores are lapped by the Atlantic Ocean, while its western boundaries are marked by the magnificent Andes. Boundary disputes between Argentina and Chile were numerous. A broadly agreed principle stated that where rivers flowed west they would be in Chile and where they flowed east they would be Argentinian. However, boundaries are always contentious and there is a saying that 'Chile is God's way of keeping Argentina from the Pacific'.[3]

In a final attempt to determine and set the boundaries, the two countries agreed that they would invite the British Crown to appoint someone to conduct an independent boundary study.

> WHEREAS, by an Agreement dated the 17th day of April 1896, the Argentine Republic and the Republic of Chile, by Their respective Representatives, determined:
>
> THAT should differences arise between their experts as to the boundary-line to be traced between the two States in conformity with the Treaty of 1881 and the Protocol of 1893, and in case such differences could not be amicably settled by accord between the two Governments, they should be submitted to the decision of the Government of Her Britannic Majesty.[4]

Sir Thomas Hungerford Holdich of the Royal Engineers, and a Vice-President of the Royal Geographical Society, was appointed as the arbiter. Sir Thomas travelled the length and breadth of the region in pursuit of a political solution that would also be realistic in terms of the terrain. Sir Thomas was an eminently qualified geographer, but it has been suggested that on more than one occasion he determined some fairly arbitrary recommendations, following the hospitality of some landowners.

Patagonia's vegetation is fit for little else but sheep, and while the many wild animals make it a land of curiosity, the climate, while hostile, had the advantage of making it relatively free from infectious diseases for the new inhabitants. The climate did not however prevent these new inhabitants to Patagonia passing on 'white man's' diseases to the native population. The range of temperature is quite extreme – between +26°C and -26°C. Yet, on closer inspection there are many small plants growing in the dusty soil. The productivity of the soil is mainly hampered by the lack of water.

One native Patagonian plant has developed its own Caithness connection; the Magellan daisy/ragwort (*Senecio smithii*), which grows in the ditches between Punta Arenas and Puerto Natales, also grows in the Dunnet area of Caithness. Allegedly it was brought back by whalers, but just which whaler, and when the plant was brought back to Dunnet, remain a mystery. Inspired by the story and its mystery, Joanne Kaar, a Caithness artist, has created a Portable Museum which explores the story.[5]

The initial push was to develop the rural and inland areas of Patagonia, yet naturally, small towns and communities were also established as economic and political interest in the region grew. Punta Arenas (Sandy Point), began to grow as a community in 1848, when the Chilean government established it as a fort and penal colony. Following some dramatic violence this was eventually abandoned.

Punta Arenas played a key role in the integration of Scots into Patagonia. Many of the Caithness Patagonian Pioneers arrived at the settlement before making their way into the Patagonian hinterland. Between 1911 and 1920, 392 Scots born in Scotland lived in the town. Positioned on the main shipping route through the Straits of Magellan, its geographic position made it a key destination. It was not until the Panama Canal opened in 1912 that its importance in shipping terms diminished. Because of its southerly location, Punta Arenas also played a key role in the expeditions to open up the Antarctic; Ernest Shackleton's Antarctic adventures had a base in Punta Arenas.

Punta Arenas attracted a colourful and diverse population. A description from early days claimed it as 'a town with pink roofs that sheltered at once the miner, the prospector, the cowboy, the lumberman and happy-go-lucky-Jack'.[6] A Mr Dick, who managed some of the Hamilton & Saunders business in Patagonia, is quoted as saying that 'Punta Arenas is worse than Wick'.

Punta Arenas also became an important trading location for the native tribes. They would exchange their furs and skins for all sorts of shiny objects. Increasingly, and to the ultimate detriment of the indigenous people, they acquired alcoholic spirits. Alcoholism became widespread among the tribes and was to be a critical element in the ultimate downfall of the proud race.

The Chilean and British navies were frequent visitors to Punta Arenas, and one British ship, the *Dotterel*, and its crew met with a violent end while anchored at the port; a fire that seems to have started in the ammunition section caused a mighty explosion that blew the ship to smithereens. One hundred and forty three men lost their lives, and as the bodies washed ashore they were buried in Punta Arenas cemetery.

Rio Gallegas grew into the most significant town on the Argentinian side of southern Patagonia. Officially it is the capital of Santa Cruz province. The town began life around 1885 as a wool port, and was described by the writer A. F. Tschiffely: 'a great many of the houses are merely shacks, covered with tin roofs and none of the streets are paved'.[7]

Rio Gallegas was also the meeting place for many farmers to conduct their business. It was here that Caithness Patagonian pioneer John Hamilton made his mark. Today the town proudly commemorates his influence in the development of sheep farming in the area with a street name – Calle Juan Hamilton.

The Argentine President, Juan Perón, spent many of his formative years in Rio Gallegas. The Perón family found themselves down on their luck in the early 1900s, so when Juan was about five years old the family moved to Rio Gallegas.

The other key eastern Patagonian towns are Puerto Deseado, San Julián and Puerto Santa Cruz. Puerto Deseado's origins can be traced back to 1883, when Juan Antonio Santiago Oneto was tasked with founding a colony at the mouth of the Deseado river. An initial group of five families led the way in the establishment of what became a key town for the export of wool and refrigerated mutton. Now, in the 21st century, Puerto Deseado is a thriving fishing town.

1 *Patagonia, A Forgotten Land: from Magellan to Perón* / C.A Brebbia. WIT Press. 2006.
2 Papers of William Alexander Blain, Shepherd in Falkland Islands, Patagonia and Tierra Del Fuego, and of His Son William J. Blain, Dalry. National Archives of Scotland – GD1/987.
3 *An Englishman in Patagonia*/ John Pilkington.1991.
4 Award by his Majesty King Edward VII in the Argentine Chile Boundary Case 20 November 1902.
5 http://joannebkaarbakersbotanistswhalers.blogspot.co.uk/p/magellan-daisy-whalers.html.
6 *The Gold Diggings of Cape Horn*/ John R. Spears.2012.
7 *The Way Southward*/ Aime Felix Tschiffely.

The New Patagonian Inhabitants

While the main influx of people into Patagonia came towards the end of the 19th century, it was from the early years of that century that Scots had been key developers and participants of business in Argentina. One English commentator claimed that the: 'majority of British merchants are natives of Scotland, proverbial for their talent and activity in trade'.[1] No great surprise, then, that Caithness people would find themselves among the leading pioneers in Patagonia. The Caithness influx to Argentina began when two Caithness brothers, James and George Waters from Thurso, are known to have migrated to Argentina around the middle of the 19th century. It appears their base was in the more northern part of Argentina, probably Buenos Aires.

The history of a concerted Scots emigration to Argentina began in 1825 with a deliberate attempt to establish a community at Monte Grande, near Buenos Aires. The ship *Symmetry* had been chartered, and departed from Leith with 220 Scots on board. The originators of the scheme were John and William Parish Robertson, who had purchased land in Argentina, aiming to capitalise on the agricultural skills of Scots, especially those from the Scottish Borders. With the agricultural equipment and supplies they brought with them, the colony at first seemed to prosper. However, when the colony found itself caught up in the middle of an Argentinian conflict, many of the people fled to Buenos Aires, leading to the ultimate breakup of the community.[2]

A further attempt to establish a Scots colony was made in November 1875, when R. Stephens & Co. of Glasgow proposed the emigration of 140 Scottish families for a settlement at Port Desire in Patagonia.[3]

Meanwhile the Welsh had been successful in establishing a unique culturally focused community. They had arrived *en masse* (about 200 migrants) in 1865 on board the *Mimosa*. Despite some significant early difficulties, which included floods, poor crops and internal disputes, they persevered in establishing a colony in Chubut province. In 1875 the Argentine government granted the community legal rights to the land.

Today their descendants continue to maintain their Welsh language and culture within the wider Argentine society. A curious aside in that connection is that an early explorer of the region had actually thought that the native people of Patagonia were of Welsh origin. And delightfully, the word 'penguin' when written in Welsh is *pen gwyn*, meaning 'white head'.

Apart from the Welsh in 1865, and the Scots in 1825 and 1875, emigration to Patagonia was a much more individually motivated decision. People from all walks of life and from across the length and breadth of Britain, sailed to Patagonia in the 19th and early 20th centuries, looking for a new life, or at the least a source of income. In time many would follow their relatives in a form of chain migration. Yet, while Caithness is hardly the most geographically obvious starting point, it did have a history of sheep and sheep farming. The great Caithness agricultural improver, Sir John Sinclair, was a considerable advocate of sheep farming and an experimenter of sheep breeding.

Emigration to new lands has often been the result of either forced servitude or a response to inducements. By the time Caithness men were making their way to Patagonia, forced servitude, thankfully, had been largely eliminated. However, the economic conditions of the times did have some influence over the decision to leave. As early as 1836 the *Inverness Journal* was reporting an exodus from Caithness due to the fishing season coming to a close. Many people at this stage were heading south for the industrial towns of both Scotland and England, although this was also a period of substantial numbers of people emigrating to North America.

In reality this was a period of economic movement. Census returns show that between 1861 and 1901 around half a million Scots emigrated, including moving to England. Employment opportunities at home in Caithness were limited, and overcrowding was not just a community problem, but was also a challenge for many large families. Seeking potentially better prospects was therefore a risk worth taking. The *Glasgow Herald* in November 1883 reported that:

> Those who can muster sufficient money and courage – more especially those who being still young and strong can adapt themselves to any kind of life they prefer – are seeking homes in other parts of the globe where there is room for them and where there is work to be done.[4]

The Argentine government of the late 19th century was actively encouraging immigration; in 1876 it passed an Immigration and Colonisation Law, with the express purpose of encouraging people to settle in the lands across Patagonia.

There was a belief in Argentina that people from northern Europe would provide a counterbalance to its domestic, and less than industrious, population.[5] The Scots in particular were viewed as desirable immigrants, as they were considered to be the most able at adapting to the environment. Most importantly, they could 'take on the habits and customs of the people with whom they will share'.[6]

The middle to late 19th century was a period of relative prosperity in Buenos Aires and northern Argentina. The Argentines were therefore less willing to take on the risk of developing Patagonia:

Several attempts to bring immigrants from Buenos Aires were made, but were unsuccessful because these men did not hesitate to reject any proposal put to them going to the South, since in central regions of the Republic were offered fertile land with good weather and easy roads.[7]

Recruiting agents were sent from the Argentine to a number of British cities, and copies of Mulhall's *Handbook of the River Plate* were being handed out in British working men's clubs. This publication:

offers a fine field for immigrants, as is proved by the thousands of Europeans here who have gained fortune and position during the last twenty years.

Among the entries in the book we find two citing John Hamilton, the Caithness pioneer, as an example of success:

from the 1850s one of the principal British *estancieros* in the Partido de Magdalena, Buenos Aires province [and] owner of one of the principal estancias in the Partido of Rivadavia, Buenos Aires province.

The British government, however, was less than supportive. Encouraging emigration outside of the British Empire was considered as a waste of resources. Better to populate and equip countries such as Canada and Australia.

Scaremongering techniques were actively used to dissuade British people from going to Argentina and Chile; for example, the British Emigration Commission in 1870 issued a warning against going to Argentina or Chile, claiming that several Britons had been murdered.[8] Posters were printed and sent to post offices and other public locations throughout Britain. The pressure was further applied in 1909 when the British government produced posters warning against emigration to Chili [*sic*], headed:

WARNING TO INTENDING EMIGRANTS

SPECIAL WARNING TO SHEPHERDS AND OTHERS[9]

The message described life in Patagonia as extremely harsh, with working conditions and wages not expected to match those at home. The Argentine government officially complained, refuting the accusations and produced statistics showing the numbers of people who had already settled. Writer and traveller Arthur Jerdein backed up the Argentine position:

*English people at home, as a rule, have a very one sided opinion re-
garding this country, and look upon it as one full of bad characters,
with no security for either life or property, and consequently unfit for
emigration. I decidedly differ ... I would just as soon invest my money
in the country as I would in either England or the United States or
Australia. The revolutions which take place from time to time do not
disturb the emigrant or capitalist in the least; the natives themselves
are the only ones to suffer.*[10]

Nonetheless, the thirst for emigration and new opportunity was strong enough
for many to disregard the advice. A society named the Emigrant and Colonist's Aid
Corporation Ltd made an offer to the Argentine government to provide the country
with 1,000 families. This scheme failed, largely because of the costs involved and
conditions imposed.

Ironically, sheep had been one of the main reasons behind the large-scale 19th-
century emigration from Scotland. Yet it was sheep that constituted the major
Patagonian attraction.

Argentina had known and valued sheep for some time:

Sheep first arrived in Argentina from Peru in 1587. The animals thrived on the
estancias of the pampas around Buenos Aires and by 1840 the numbers of sheep
were equal to the number of cattle raised on the pampas. In 1852 there were seven
sheep for every human being; by the late 1880s the ratio had increased to 30:1. In
1888 Argentina had 87 million sheep – more than any other country in the world.[11]

By the late 19th century, Patagonia was recognised as a viable addition to
Argentinian sheep production, and while initial sheep stocks were brought from
the north, the neighbouring Falkland Islands also became an important source for
Patagonian sheep farmers. John Hamilton from Wick via the Falkland Islands, once
established in Patagonia, was instrumental in attracting shepherds from Caithness.
He is quoted as encouraging Mauricio Braun and Jose Menendez to recruit Scottish
shepherds. Hamilton suggested to Menendez that the best method of recruiting
Scottish shepherds would be to place an advertisement in the Scottish newspapers.
Menendez however, chose to place his advertisements in *The Scotsman* rather than
the more provincial newspapers. The result was a spate of applications from clerks,
etc. and not from those experienced in shepherding.

Hamilton's own advertisements in the Caithness newspaper, the *John O'Groat
Journal*, offered fixed-term contracts with passage out and back home. This must
have provided some measure of security, but it also suggests that there was an
expectation that some would indeed return home to Caithness.

One of the Hamilton recruits was John Cormack, from Achow near Lybster in Caithness. In 1904 he was employed on the Hamilton & Saunders estancia, Punta Loyola. Alongside learning the skills of Patagonian sheep farming, he was able to use his carpentry skills. Woodworking skills were in considerable demand in the early years on the expanding estancias; buildings were required to accommodate the increasing sheep farming operations and the growing numbers of people. Those with carpentry skills were also called upon to construct household furniture. A number of the Caithness men such as George Bain and Robert Nicolson were known to have been adept at joinery.

Many of the Caithness Patagonian Pioneers ultimately settled in Patagonia. Today there are a number of Patagonian residents who are the direct descendants of these early Caithness Pioneers. Others returned to Caithness, bringing both good and bad memories with them.

1 *Scots in Argentina and Patagonia Austral 1800–1950/* Arnold Morrison.
2 *Records of the Scottish Settlers in the River Plate and their Churches/* Dodds, James. Grant and Sylvester, 1897.
3 Immigration policy & settlement: the example of British immigration into late 19th-century Argentina in *The Forgotten Colony: A History of the English Speaking Communities in Argentina/* Andrew Graham-Yooll.
4 *Glasgow Herald* 14 November 1883.
5 *Argentina: a modern history/* Jill Hedges. 2011.
6 *The British in Santa Cruz territory 1911–2011/* María de los Milagros Pierini and Pablo Gustavo Beecher. Edición del Club Británico de Río Gallegos
7 *Los extranjeros en la conformación de la élite Santa Cruceña/*Guenaga, 1994: 9.
8 Immigration policy & settlement: the example of British immigration into late 19th century Argentina in *The Forgotten Colony: A History of the English Speaking Communities in Argentina/* Andrew Graham-Yooll.
9 National Archives of Scotland – HH1/2247.
10 *The Argentine Republic as a Field for the Agriculturist, the Stock Farmer and the Capitalist/* Arthur Jerdein, 1870.
11 *Dusk on the Campo/*Sara Mansfield Taber. Henry Holt 1992.

The Land They Left Behind

Land has always preoccupied the minds of Scotland's people – owning it, working it, or simply being cleared off it. The infamous Highland Clearances created a new land ownership structure, which had little or no place for many of the original inhabitants. In general, the new landlord class in the Highlands of Scotland put profit before people, leaving many families either displaced or destitute. Caithness was not immune to the Clearances, although in truth it provided a haven for many of those who had been 'cleared' from the straths of Sutherland. The crofts and small landholdings scattered across the Caithness and Sutherland boundary areas became home to many of the displaced. Nineteenth-century Caithness also benefited from the boom in herring fishing, so employment was available to Caithness people and to many from across the Highlands and Islands.

Caithness was also the centre of a thriving flagstone industry. At its height, it employed about 1,000 men.[1] So while times were hard and families were large, it was not all gloom. People were close to a limited form of self-sufficiency; they grew their own crops and reared their own, albeit limited, livestock. For other necessities of life, they turned to neighbours in their communities – tailors, dressmakers, shoemakers, blacksmiths and so on.

Both the fishing and flagstone industries began to decline by the end of the 19th century. Fishing in particular created a number of ancillary industries but with the downturn in it came a consequent loss of wages. This in turn created difficulties in meeting the costs of living. Rents, of course, continued to rise; the Clyth Estate, for example, was the home to a number of Caithness Patagonian pioneer families, and rents on the estate had almost doubled between the 1860s and the 1880s. As a direct result, emigration increased.

The population of Caithness in 1861 was about 40,000 and by the time that the first of the Caithness Patagonian Pioneers had left, it is estimated that somewhere between 100 and 150 people per annum were leaving Caithness.[2]

In 1901 the population of Caithness had fallen to about 34,000, proof that the area was, either not able to support its young population, or that the lure of better prospects was becoming much more viable.

While major steps were taken to combat illness in all parts of Scotland through inoculation schemes and advice on healthy living conditions, illness still affected many families. The Pulteneytown Academy School Logbook for 1875 records the consequences of a scarlet fever outbreak.; five of the school's pupils died, and as a measure to try to prevent the spread, all schools in Wick were closed for a period.[3] John Hamilton's brother Andrew was a victim of the disease.

The Bain family from Mavesy lost two sons – Robert aged two and Angus aged three – both died from measles in 1887, caught up in the epidemic that was sweeping Caithness at the time. It was reckoned that 500 children in Wick alone were absent from school on account of the illness.[4] Even as late as 1907, Lannergill School was closed for a period due to an outbreak of measles. Ironically, measles was to become a major killer amongst the native Patagonians.

Caithness, like many other areas of Scotland, had been victim to the killer disease cholera. While its worst effects had passed by the time the Caithness Patagonian Pioneers were growing up, stringent prevention conditions were still in force in the late 1890s. A prohibition order existed in 1890, preventing the landing of ships from Spain, due to the continuing prevalence of the disease in parts of Spain. In 1892 there were 66 cases of non-specified infectious diseases reported in Caithness, so vigilance was critical.

The medical services in Caithness were probably little different from those in the rest of Scotland. Yet it was not until 1893 that the first nurse was appointed in Wick. The doctors throughout Caithness at that time numbered 14.[5] Long-term care provision, especially for those with mental illness, was very limited.

Staff at Dunbar Hospital in Thurso looked after some elderly patients, but those requiring more long-term support and treatment were often admitted to Sunnyside Royal Hospital much further south, in Montrose. Significant numbers of Caithness patients can be found among the Sunnyside patient lists, including two of the Hamilton family. Jessie (née Cormack), wife of David Bain, also ended her days at Sunnyside after returning from Patagonia. The hospital had originally operated under the name of Montrose Royal Asylum and was the designated facility for the private and health care patients from Caithness who required longer-term care. The local authorities were responsible for the upkeep payments for those in more 'humble' circumstances; Caithness County Council was charged £48 per annum for Caithness residents.

A doubling up of medical functions was not uncommon in Caithness. For example, in Thurso dentistry was carried out by the druggist, William Bremner – not that he used any drugs. He extracted teeth, often in public, on the pavement in front of his shop. Two assistants held the patient firmly in a chair while Bremner hauled out the offending molar, which he then displayed to the admiring spectators.[6]

Public health was an issue still facing Caithness at the end of the 19th century. In 1891 the Caithness Public Health Committee passed a resolution that enabled the sanitary inspector to report on any houses held by and occupied by farm servants as part of their wages. Over the next few years a number of insanitary orders were served on a range of these accommodations, and as a result a general raising of standards regarding housing in Caithness did lead to an improvement. The old-style building which accommodated humans and their beasts was being replaced with separate stone-built dwellings and byres. There remained however, a preponderance of large families living in cramped conditions. How many of our Caithness Patagonian Pioneers simply left home to get some space? If that was the case, they certainly found space in Patagonia!

Nineteenth-century education in Caithness was based on a mix of regulation, need and opportunity. Attendance at many of the rural schools was determined firstly by the weather and secondly by the needs of the family; school logbooks detail a litany of summer days when few pupils attended. The children were often employed in some aspect of the harvest or other farm-related work. Caithness Patagonian pioneer Angus McPherson, along with a number of his fellow pupils, left Spittal School to work as herds[7] over the summer months. In May 1888, the headmaster noted: 'A good few of the older pupils have left school for summer work … I will report them to the Officer.'

By November 1888, the headmaster was able to report: 'Most of the herds have now returned to school but find they are very far back with their work for the Standards.'[8]

In winter the problem revolved around the weather conditions; heavy snowfall was a relatively common cause of school closure. The Lannergill School logbook, however, provides evidence of reasons why other lessons were missed: 'There was no sewing on Tuesday, Wednesday or Thursday. The sewing mistress being confined to bed.'[9]

Even when attendance was good, the extent of the space available presented another challenge. The Newlands School Logbook has the following entry for 1876: 'School crowded almost to suffocation. Had window down. Difficult to keep order. Scholars half delirious before 4 o'clock.'

Nevertheless, education was important to the people of Caithness. During the period when John Hamilton started school in Wick, a number of schools existed in the town: Wick Parish School in Kirkhill was established in 1869; and the Free Church in Wick ran two schools at that time, one in Stafford Lane, the other at the corner of MacRae Street. The largest of the town's schools, Pulteneytown Academy, was built in 1839. Two 'ragged' schools for the children of paupers existed – one off the High Street, the other in Miller Street.[10]

The passing of the Education Act of 1872 made schooling compulsory for all children aged between 5 and 13 in Scotland. The Act also forced the amalgamation of some schools and the building of new schools throughout Caithness, for example Wick West Banks School, which opened in 1877. This was a period of increasing literacy among much of the populace. In Wick, through the services of publisher and bookseller Peter Reid, access to the novels of Scott and Dickens were among the available literary options.

So our Caithness Patagonian Pioneers were not without education. The geography of the world was most definitely on the curriculum of Caithness schools. The new owners of a converted Caithness country school found, on taking ownership, a large map of the world on what had been the classroom wall. John Hamilton and the other Caithness Patagonian Pioneers would have grown up knowing at least the location of Argentina and Chile in relation to the rest of the world. This newspaper quote from 1865 confirms the success of teaching geography:

> A remarkably well executed chart from England to the Cape Verde Islands has been made by one of the pupils of Mr Brass's navigation class at Staxigoe. It is admirably finished in colours with an ornamental border of the flags of the nations.[11]

More than geography was being taught in the Caithness schools. Angus McPherson, on arrival in Patagonia, began writing a series of diaries. Written with some literary skill and peppered with quotes from Robert Burns, these diaries are a testimony to the education Angus received at Spittal School in Caithness. Angus was one of ten children, who all followed different trajectories in life, and while their parents were of modest means and probably classed as illiterate, Angus, like his siblings, carved out a successful field of employment.

Caithness was in many respects at the forefront of sheep farming. Sir John Sinclair, the agricultural improver, was a leader and enthusiast in terms of animal husbandry. He introduced and experimented with new sheep breeds on his Langwell Estate. Apparently, when attempting to introduce Merinos, he found that they did not fare well in wet weather, so he equipped his flock with leather boots. But it was his introduction of the Cheviot breed that was to have the greatest impact on sheep farming in Caithness and throughout the Highlands of Scotland. Here was a breed that suited the development of sheep farming on the huge scale required.

By the late 19th century, farming in Caithness was a mix of arable farms and crofts. Employment in Patagonia was largely in the sheep farming industry, and many of the Caithness Patagonian Pioneers had backgrounds in farming. Some were the sons of shepherds, with experience of Caithness sheep farming. The scale of operations they met in Patagonia must have been at first bewildering.

The people of Caithness benefited only marginally from the leisure opportunities becoming more readily available to those in Scotland's larger towns. Distance and access were major barriers to the people of Caithness, but a railway link with the rest of the country was finally completed in 1874. Up until then, shipping had been the major communication route. Regular steamers sailed between Wick and Leith, but while they did carry passengers, their main purpose was cargo. Wherever Caithness people sought to go, they had firstly to make a long journey south. This particularly applied to the Caithness Patagonian Pioneers, who sailed to Patagonia from either Liverpool or Southampton. Within Caithness, a railway link between Lybster and

Wick was opened in 1903, opening up opportunities for those in the Lybster area to visit Wick on special occasions. The Wick and Lybster railway also provided a lifeline for many in Wick; on 28 May 1922, Wick voted to become a dry town, with no alcohol licences being allowed. Lybster on the other hand welcomed those in need of a dram.

1 *The Caithness Book*/Donald Omand. Highland Printers. 1973.
2 *The Wick and Lybster Light Railway*/ Iain Sutherland. 1987.
3 Pulteneytown Academy Log Book Caithness Archive Centre – CC/5/3/60/4.
4 *Scottish Highlander* 27/10/1887.
5 *Amulets to Isotopes: a history of medicine in Caithness*/ D H A Boyd. John Donald 1998.
6 *Amulets to Isotopes: a history of medicine in Caithness*/ D. H. A. Boyd. John Donald 1998.
7 Common usage to define the job.
8 Spittal School Log Book – Caithness Archive Centre CC/5/2/23/4.
9 Lannergill School Log Book – Caithness Archive Centre CC/5/3/56/2.
10 *The Caithness Book*/ Donald Omand. Highland Printer.1973.
11 *The Caithness Book*/ Donald Omand. Highland Printer.1973.

The Journey

Caithness to Patagonia was a mammoth journey. The earliest of the Caithness Patagonian Pioneers could, after arriving in Liverpool, expect a journey of some seven weeks between boarding there and arriving in Punta Arenas.

John Hamilton left for the Falkland Islands in 1880, while others from Caithness headed to Patagonia in the early 1890s. In an interview with travel writer John Pilkington, Margaret Harper, the daughter of John Harper from Wick, mentions that it took her mother 70 days to sail from Liverpool to the Falkland Islands. James Nicol from Clashach in Caithness, while he did not go to Patagonia, did sail for the Falklands in 1879, and his diary charts a journey that took from January to March of that year.

Perhaps, all was not too bad! Tom Jones in his book *Patagonian Panorama* recounts his initial journey from Liverpool to Punta Arenas, telling the reader that at their first port of call, La Pallice, the ship took on board three prostitutes bound for Buenos Aires. Other forms of leisure were also required to pass away the weeks on board. Wrestling was apparently one of the sports that the Bain brothers liked to engage in. Angus Robert Bain in particular, seems to have been something of a champion at the sport, no doubt due to his considerable strength; a family memory tells of Angus Robert stopping a runaway train on the Wick–Lybster Railway when, a carriage having apparently come off the track, Angus grabbed a log and threw it under the carriage, thus bringing the train to a halt.

Liverpool and Southampton Docks must have been something of an eye-opener for those making their first trip abroad. James Nicol from Clashach departed in 1879 for the Falkland Islands, and he records in his diary that he was somewhat awestruck by the size of the ships. After London, Liverpool was the second biggest port of the British Empire, and it was the main gateway for goods and passengers heading west. At the time the first of the Caithness pioneers were setting sail for South America, Liverpool docks employed some 30,000 workers. However busy Wick harbour had been during the herring fishing boom years, this was life on another scale.

The Liverpool departures generally took emigrants to Punta Arenas, the main port for southern Patagonia. As Buenos Aires became a destination option, Southampton, or on occasion London, became the main ports of departure. The ships of the time did not simply travel non-stop between the two ports, so for many the journey would have given them sight of Lisbon and other ports. The aforesaid James Nicol, on his way to the Falklands, took the Montevideo route calling in along the coasts of Spain and Portugal, allowing him the opportunity to comment on the villages and coastline that could be seen from the ship. Port Stanley in the Falkland Islands was also a staging post for those travelling onward to Punta Arenas. The descendants of John Munro have a postcard sent home from Vilagarcia in Spain while *en route* to Patagonia.[1]

Of course the journey started way before Liverpool, Southampton or London.

The first part of the journey was the mental one – the decision to go! The motives are largely unknown, but can be guessed. Large families and crowded homes encouraged people to find their own spaces and places. The lack of employment and income would have motivated some. Maybe there was a general dissatisfaction with life in Caithness and a new adventure offered the hope of a better future. Hope over fear may have driven many, literally throwing their fate to the winds. Recruitment campaigns, as we have seen, were initiated, and advertisements began to appear in the press.

The *Scottish Highlander*, a northern Scotland-based newspaper, carried advertisements from 1888 such as this:

Shepherds wanted immediately (young men) for Straits of Magellan. Five years engagement. Wages £50 to £60. Free Passage. Apply to Grant & Co, Shipping Agents, 21 Inglis Street, Inverness.[2]

Grant & Co. continued to run these advertisements at least through to 1890. In 1891 we find John Hamilton recruiting in Caithness:

Wanted Shepherds – a few single young men for Patagonia, South America. Five years engagement, wages £30 first year, rising to £60 last year. Passage paid out and home and keep found during whole tenure of engagement. Apply personally by letter to James Hamilton, Clothier, 52 Dempster Street, Pulteneytown, Wick.[3]

Formal recruitment apart, Caithness is a relatively small place, and many people knew, or knew of, men who had made their way to Patagonia. Robert Nicolson's regular trips back to Lybster would have provided an opportunity for others to be impressed enough to consider Patagonia. James Mackay from Geislittle listened to the stories and consequently gained a position on Robert Nicolson's Patagonian estancia. In other instances, brothers, sons and nephews followed. William Bain's four brothers and two sisters followed him to Patagonia. Andrew Harper came home from Patagonia on a visit in 1906, having spent eight or nine years there, and two months later his brother Robert sailed back to Patagonia with him. Alexander and George Plowman must have been sufficiently impressed by the experiences of their father, James Plowman, to go to Patagonia. John Munro followed his uncles, Hugh and Angus McPherson, to Patagonia.

Once the decision was made, the Caithness men and women had to make the lengthy journey to Liverpool or Southampton – bear in mind that the railway south was only opened in 1874. By the time some of the early pioneers were leaving (1890s), even with the railway, this remained something of a novel and possibly arduous, experience. Advertisements in the *John O'Groat Journal* for 1880 show that a train leaving Wick at 11.30 a.m. arrived in London at 8.00 p.m. the next day. The cost was 82s 8d. Even in 1920 it took eight and a half hours to go from Wick to Inverness. It was not until the 1930s that it was possible to make a trip from Caithness to London by motor coach, so road transport was not a realistic option for the earliest Caithness Patagonian Pioneers. One option was to go by sea at least part of the way. There were regular sailings between Wick and Leith. From there the transport options further south would have opened up.

Next was the seven-week sea trip with the potential monotony that this could entail. The shipping records show that on many occasions Caithness emigrants to Patagonia travelled together; for example Nicol Oman sailed with Angus Robert Bain. For some, though, the journey without friends must have been more of an ordeal. Jessie Lizzie Bain from Lybster sailed from Liverpool to Punta Arenas in September 1914 to join her brothers. Shepherds from the Western Isles were also moving to Patagonia,[4] and a number of Lewis-based shepherds were on board, but there do not appear to have been any other Caithness people accompanying Jessie on the ship.

While no mention is made of dogs in John Hamilton's recruiting advertisements, in some instances it was apparently a requirement that the emigrating shepherds should bring with them an appropriate sheepdog. Those Patagonian-bound from the Western Isles were required to take two dogs with them. Obviously, there was no way that any prize dog was going to be allowed to leave the home croft, but legend has it that when the men arrived at Liverpool ready to sail, they spent their final night ashore kidnapping any mongrel they could find on Liverpool's streets. A family memory claims that brothers John and Nicol Oman did indeed take their dogs with them to Patagonia. Perhaps John Hamilton also brought a dog with him; his descendants recount that a Patagonian puma killed his best dog.

There would have been little opportunity to transport much more than a few personal items and clothing. Descendants of the Caithness Patagonian Pioneers recall that a bible would have featured among their limited possessions. Potentially for those who returned home to marry, the return trip would have included some items of cutlery, crockery and other household goods. Again descendants recall that on these post- marriage trips the wedding presents would be among their possessions. How practical some of these things would have been remains doubtful. The second *Beagle* expedition brought, as gifts the likes of 'crockery sets, chamber pots, glasses, cutlery and many other objects equally unsuitable for the realities of living in Tierra del Fuego'.[5]

The Pacific Steam Navigation Company was the first to initiate regular sailings to Punta Arenas. By 1873 it had the largest merchant steamer fleet in the world, consisting of 57 vessels. In 1908 it introduced larger luxury passenger liners[6] such as the *Orcoma*, which was built on Clydeside; the newly wedded William Bain and Elizabeth Sinclair experienced its relative luxury, as they returned to Patagonia in September 1910. In 1912, David Christian and his family sailed on the *Orcoma* from Punta Arenas to Liverpool. But the first of the Caithness Patagonian Pioneers, John McKinnon, William Begg and the Christian brothers David and Donald, sailed on the SS *James Watt*, a cargo ship which would have been, without doubt, somewhat less luxurious.

1 Thanks to the Munro family for making this postcard available.
2 *Scottish Highlander* 31 May 1888.
3 *John O Groat Journal* of 21 April 1891.
4 *Return to Patagonia/* Greta Mackenzie. Islands Book Trust 2011.
5 *Patagonia, A Forgotten Land: from Magellan to Perón /* C.A Brebbia. WIT Press. 2006.
6 http://www.liverpoolmuseums.org.uk/maritime/archive/sheet/14.

The Land They Came To

As a nation state, Argentina effectively came into being in 1816, with its Declaration of Independence removing itself from Spanish control. Chile declared its independence from Spain in 1818. The region of Patagonia is shared between Chile and Argentina; in the south of Argentina lie the Patagonian provinces of Chubut and Santa Cruz – a long way from the seat of power in Buenos Aires. The territory of Santa Cruz was created in 1884 and declared a province in 1957. To this day, Patagonia remains not just geographically but politically isolated from the north of Argentina.

Patagonia is a vast, open and largely flat landscape. With strong winds and little rainfall, the land is desertlike. The annual rainfall in Patagonia averages between 100 and 400 mm (4–16 inches), with wide variations from coastal areas to inland regions. While transport and access is now much improved from the early pioneering days, the wide and desolate expanses of Patagonia as you travel across it still take your breath away. Surely these first Caithness Patagonian Pioneers must have had some idea of what to expect – yet there seems little doubt that what they found must have been something of an eye-opening experience: 'Nature must have made Patagonia last of all her works'.[1]

It is difficult from our 21st century perspective to find a challenge that might compare with the step into the relative unknown taken by the Caithness Patagonian Pioneers; except perhaps emigration to a moon base? They faced a land not just of vastness but also of isolation and extreme weather conditions. Distances were described in leagues, but it seems the term could vary as to its actual length. An early traveller in Patagonia, Florence Dixie, wrote of her experience in 1879:

> We found that the idea of a league was mostly elastic, appearing to vary daily ... Thus a league might mean ten miles today and tomorrow, possibly only one.[2]

The first sight of land after a sea crossing lasting up to seven weeks would have been one of thankfulness for a journey's end, and possibly one of wonderment at the surrounding shorelines. Sailing into the Strait of Magellan would have been an experience in itself.

The strait is notorious in the history of the search for a route between the Atlantic and Pacific Oceans. At most it is 22 miles wide, and it narrows to only 1.9 miles, giving travellers ample opportunity to view the rocky coastline. The names of some of the places however might have filled the pioneers with some dread. The coast of Patagonia is rich in 'well named' places – Useless Bay; Desolation Island; Gulf of Troubles; Last Hope Sound, Port Famine and so on.

The initial port of call for many was Punta Arenas at the southern tip of Chile. At the time of the first pioneer arrivals, it was little more than a ramshackle collection of huts but it nevertheless rapidly became a haven for travellers on many different missions. The town's history is one of conflict. Punta Arenas had begun life as a military open prison, but the prison compound and much of the town was destroyed during a revolt in 1852.

Around that time, Punta Arenas contained around 50 houses and some 700 people, about half of them convicted prisoners. Described by one of John Hamilton's managers as a town 'worse than Wick', it was to descend into a period of chaos as both inmates and soldiers rioted. The town of Ushuaia on nearby Tierra del Fuego had also been established as a penal colony, this time by the Argentinians; both prisons were used mainly for the detention of dangerous criminals. Escapes from the prison in Punta Arenas were frequent, with regular manhunts mounted to recapture the escapees, but the remoteness of the location was a major consideration in the decision to riot.

Punta Arenas gradually began to be rebuilt, and by 1875 the first British consul, John J Hamilton, (no connection) was in residence. Given its location, Punta Arenas was a natural centre for the development of the support industries needed to service the developing sheep farming. Banks, transport and other ancillary services grew up within Punta Arenas. However, once again in 1877, the town was the victim of an army revolt, with many of its buildings reduced to ashes.

As transport across the Atlantic improved, Argentina's capital city became more attractive to the more established Caithness Patagonians, who were now able to make trips to and from Scotland.

Buenos Aires in 1900 was one of the richest cities in the world. Trade in beef and grain from the country's rich northern lands helped make the city a major hub. Those arriving and departing from Buenos Aires must have been impressed by the bustle. Beyond the port, Buenos Aires was also a city of high energy. Music and dance has always been at the heart of the birthplace of the tango.

Once in Patagonia, the Caithness Pioneers would have been confronted with a range of animals with no equivalent in the north of Scotland. Patagonia is home to a range of exotic and in some cases fierce animals. Across the interior of the region roam herds of guanaco, a llama-type creature that was an important source of food and clothing. From the guanaco came the hides that went to make the gaucho's[3] lasso, reins, bolas[4] and shoes. Guanaco tendons were also the source for the making of arrows. The indigenous women were very clever at sewing, despite the primitive clumsiness of their tools; their needles consisted of pieces of bone sharpened to a point, and the thread they used was made from guanaco sinews. The skins went to form the basis of the warm capas: 'The capa is a long robe of guanaco furs about five and a half feet long by four and a half broad.'[5]

Guanaco flesh was a main food source. In spite of being hunted and killed in numbers, they have remained inquisitive about humans, yet when they are startled or alarmed they make a sound like a kind of 'derisive laugh'. One guanaco in a herd seems to act as a guard and alerts the rest when danger threatens.[6]

The rhea, an ostrich-like flightless bird, was described by John Pilkington as 'skittish and cowardly'. They too were an important source of food, and their eggs stay fresh for up to six months. Rheas nest in a hole in the ground, under a bush, and if hunters were lucky, they could find upwards of 40 eggs in a nest. Care of the rheas' nests and eggs are the responsibility of the male birds.

The scourge of the sheep farmer was the puma or mountain lion, measuring up to 10 feet in length. They happily killed sheep way beyond their own food needs. This was particularly true of the female pumas when teaching their young to hunt and kill. The male pumas tended to kill to eat, whereas the mother and cubs would, having killed, eat just the limbs of sheep and lambs. The female puma would herd a number of sheep into a circle and along with her cubs begin the slaughter, killing up to some 30 or 40 sheep in one night, which she then stores under a grass cover. Farmers learned to spot these grassy mounds and would inject the sheep carcasses with arsenic. When the puma returned for its next dinner that would also be its last – although it took some time to perfect the correct amounts of poison; in some of the early instances the dose simply made the puma sick! A more modern approach to keeping the pumas away from the sheep is being used on Estancia Morro Chico by John Hamilton's great-grandson, Stephen Gallie. He was having a significant problem with pumas killing his sheep, so he has introduced a number of Pyrenean mountain dogs as guards. From the pup stages, the dogs are slowly introduced to the sheep, building up a relationship between the two to the extent that they happily live together. The breed has long been used by shepherds in Spain and can be trained to live among the sheep as a puma deterrent. The results in terms of sheep losses at Morro Chico have been spectacular.

However, the puma rarely attacks humans unless severely provoked, and they have been known to make playful pets if caught young; Caithness Patagonian pioneer Hugh McPherson reputedly reared a pet puma.

In the more southern reaches of the Magellanes, especially around Otway Sound, there is a large colony of Magellanic penguins. Argentina is also home to the largest rodent in the world, the capybara (also known as the carpincho). This too is a favourite meal for the puma. The human use of the carpincho is to make beautiful soft, waterproof gloves from their skins. More of a challenge for the puma is the armadillo, with its armoured shell and ability to run and burrow with some speed – but the armadillo has for centuries suffered the indignity of being eaten by humans and having its shells turned into dishes.

1 *Wanderings in Patagonia*/ Julius Beerbohm. 1881.
2 *Across Patagonia*/ Lady Florence Dixie. 1880.
3 The indigenous mounted herdsmen; later, the same, but of unspecified ethnic origin.
4 A set of cords with weights at their ends, thrown in a spinning motion to entangle the legs of an animal and bring it down.
5 *Wanderings in Patagonia*/ Julius Beerbohm. 1881.
6 *The Outermost Parts of the Earth*/ E Lucas Bridges. 1947.

The Original Patagonian Inhabitants

People have lived in Patagonia for many thousands of years. The coming of European sheep farmers to their territories was hardly welcome.

The history of the discovery, and the attempted conquering of the minds and bodies of the native people of Patagonia, was one of significant failure. Attempts to 'civilise' them included taking four young Fuegians from Tierra del Fuego to England and 'educating' them in the 'best British tradition'. The three that survived were returned to their homeland – only to revert to their native traditions. Religious missions were also established as an attempt to persuade the people of Patagonia to adopt the Christian faith, but many of these attempts ended with the abandonment of the missions. It was the coming of the sheep that forever changed the way of life of the Patagonian native inhabitants.

The native population on occasion created a challenge to the pioneers

It was a simple story of incredible hardships, battles against storm, snow, ice and hazards innumerable, but the worst enemy had been the Indians, who had apparently made steady depredations on the widely scattered flocks.[1]

In defence of the native population, their existence depended on the killing of animals for food. Sheep simply offered a relatively easy alternative, and one chief is reputed to have said: 'Everything is guanaco: a sheep is a small guanaco: a horse is a large guanaco'.[2]

The expansion of sheep farming across Patagonia and the subsequent fencing of the lands forced the native guanaco to move to higher ground, making it more difficult to hunt. The guanaco was of course the vital foodstuff and clothing source for the indigenous population, so they too were pushed into more desolate areas. The fencing also needed a wire low enough to prevent small sheep and lambs from straying beyond the farm and into easy reach of the native population.

But the early pioneers did learn from, and co-exist with, the native population. A story is told of how the Hope family (Bain descendants) found an abandoned Indian child, cared for it, and gave it 'hope'. When the child became a man, he went to war for Britain.

Given what some of the white men were doing to the indigenous people, it is unsurprising that they should seek some form of revenge. In reality, of course, these were probably fairly isolated cases, whereas in many more instances the native population and the incoming farmers were at least on tolerant terms; John Hamilton on the 'great trek' encountered an Indian camp where they were able to meet and share food, and John Cormack's daughter recalled a number of the Tehuelche tribe being given bread as they passed their farm.

There existed different tribes across Patagonia, and one of the most unusual was the Canoe People of Tierra del Fuego. They simply lived in their canoes, with a small fire burning continuously in the bottom of their boats.

Many of the early pioneers lived among, or alongside, the native Tehuelche tribes. These were a nomadic people whose lifestyle and survival depended on the seasons and the natural resources of the land. The early pioneers learned ways of survival from the native inhabitants, and in many cases strong bonds were built. Julius Beerbohm in his *Wanderings in Patagonia* found the native people far from savage:

> But I must say that in general intelligence, gentleness of temper, chastity of conduct and conscientious behaviour in social and domestic relations, they are immeasurably superior ... to the general run of civilised white men.

However, as more and more sheep began to be introduced to the great estancias, divisions began to appear between the native population and the newcomers. Many in Scotland had learned, earlier in the 19th century, that sheep and native inhabitants do not go together. The consequences of the years of the Great Sheep in the Highlands of Scotland was dislocation and relocation of the people – here in Patagonia the local population were not so 'lucky'.

Hunting the natives was to become the norm, especially in Tierra del Fuego. This was partly based on fear and ignorance of the native population, but ultimately the killing was sanctioned on economic terms. The farmers wanted to protect their lands and their profits, and they perceived that the indigenous people would simply destroy their assets. As a result 'men of British stock and extraction'[3] mercilessly hounded the native people. A current Patagonian family tells of their Scottish ancestor who first made the trip to Patagonia in response to an advertisement recruiting 'men to shoot wild beasts'. The 'wild beasts' in this case were actually the people of the native population, and to the credit of this pioneer, once the nature of the task was discovered, he refused to take part and set off to find a way back home.

This approach to native inhabitants was not unique to Patagonia. One Anne Grant, who observed at first hand the treatment meted out to Canada's native population, described the thinking: 'Calling people savages [meant that] then their blood is of no value, and their lives of no consequence.'

Some Patagonian natives undoubtedly stole sheep and especially made themselves a nuisance by cutting wire fences, but the incoming population unknowingly introduced diseases, deliberately introduced alcohol and wilfully slaughtered many. Whisky, gin and rum were exchanged for furs, feathers and gold nuggets – but it was the invidious decision to deliberately set about exterminating the native race, that was the most horrendous.

To encourage the slaughter, bounties were offered. It seems that the going rate varied depending on the rate of success. The stakes were raised when initial efforts proved to be failing. An 'Indian's' bow and arrow (their prize possession) was initially considered evidence enough that the threat was gone – but this of course did not remove the person, so the going rate changed to a pair of ears in exchange for £1. Death, however, did not necessarily follow, so: 'the system was changed and a pound sterling was paid for a head, testicles, breasts or some other vital organ'.[4]

The basic equipment carried for the hunt was a Winchester rifle, a revolver and a gaucho knife – a long and fierce instrument. The £1 was also paid upon capture alive and delivery to the Salesian church mission on Dawson Island in the Strait of Magellan, where the victim would be 'educated' and 'civilised'. At the time, many sheep farmers saw little wrong with this approach, but as news of the slaughter spread, so too did the growing condemnation.

In 1928, following the publication of a book on the subject of the killings, Argentine newspapers began to take an interest. The book accused many of the sheep farmers of being, at least, complicit in the killings. Copies of the book are scarce today, but recent research by Jose Luis Alonso Marchante has uncovered the originals written by Alberto de Agostini, a Salesian priest. Some sections of the book had been removed from later copies – among them, statements such as this: 'Explorers, ranchers and soldiers had no qualms about downloading [their] mauser against the unhappy Indians.'[5]

Marchante claims that the early Salesian priests tried to protect the native people, but as time passed the priests became more economically and financially dependent on the incoming farmers. It was from this point that the story of the massacres began to be either removed or retold in a different light.

One of the main operators in the killing of the native people of Patagonia was Alexander MacLennan, a native of Scotland, known as 'the Red Pig'. His life and times are somewhat clouded, but it is claimed that he was employed by Jose Menéndez as foreman at Estancia Primara Argentina, a sheep farm south of the Rio Grande. MacLennan led an eventful life – wounded by an arrow, then becoming an unlikely Justice of the Peace in Rio Grande in 1906, before retiring to Punta Arenas where, maybe not surprisingly, he suffered hallucinations about Indians with arrows. According to the book *Menéndez: King of Patagonia*, MacLennan was gifted an expensive watch at the end of his contract. He died in 1917.

The native tribes of Patagonia were not exempt from applying their own cruel methods of torture. Peeling the soles of the feet of anyone taken prisoner was designed to minimise the risk of them running away.

There is no evidence to suggest that any of the Caithness Pioneers were in any way involved in these actions. In fact, few of the Caithness settlers were based in Tierra del Fuego, where much of the slaughter took place. The Chilean government did initiate an enquiry into the alleged killings and issued a report in 1897, which included this statement:

> It would be unrealistic and impracticable to apply to native peoples the same rights and responsibilities that are applicable to the 'civilised' portion of society.[6]

Very jaundiced views about the indigenous inhabitants were prevalent among the incoming population, so it is little wonder that the natives' demise was little short of inevitable. Walter Young, a banker from London on a visit to Punta Arenas, wrote this unholy description of the native inhabitants:

> *These filthy savages are copper-coloured beasts with black matted hair, whose nits and generally active insect life give them, in their bored moments, plenty of industrious amusement. They live on fish-offal, hence their marine aroma; unless you had a very bad cold in your head, you could not miss them in the dark at fifty or sixty yards' distance. The women were disgusting objects and absolutely no class; their breasts seemed to have no interest in life and hung flaccidly below their knees, for the poor things knew not how to improve their figures with a straight-fronted corset.[7]*

The native peoples were not the only ones to be hunted. There existed a number of Lebanese immigrants who set themselves up as travellers and traders. They became known as 'Turks' and there are many stories of them being both tricked and killed.

It was not only the new inhabitants that sought to displace the native peoples. Various Argentinian presidents and governments saw fit to use the army against their own people, and while much of this played out politically in Buenos Aires and the more northern regions, Patagonia's native population certainly felt the effect at first hand. A military campaign during the 1870s saw General Roca's army kill some 15,000 indigenous people or displace them from their native lands.

Depending on the point of view, this was either the prelude to bringing civilisation to Patagonia or simply genocide. The basic aim of this policy was to open up Patagonia to economic development, in terms of farming.

The final insult for the native people was the setting up of closed reservations in the lands they had once roamed freely. The aim was to change their ways of thinking and acting in a manner that would make them an 'industrious and polished people'.

1 Maga's Log – *Blackwood's Magazine* Dec 1933.
2 *Patagonia, A Forgotten Land: from Magellan to Perón* / C.A Brebbia. WIT Press. 2006.
3 *Twentieth Century Impressions of Argentina*, 1911.
4 *La Patagonia Tragica/* Jose Maria Borrero.
5 El genocidio de indígenas en el sur de Chile que la historia oficial intentó ocultar.
6 http://patlibros.org/veja/?lan=eng.
7 *A Merry Banker in the Far East (and South America)/* Walter H Young.1916.

Sheep

By the mid-19th century, Scots, and indeed people from Caithness, had been emigrating to Argentina for some time. It was not only sheep that attracted people to the country. Two brothers by the name of Waters from Thurso left home for northern Argentina in the 1850s, and William Earsman, whose brothers James and Percy had settled in southern Patagonia, arrived in Argentina to work on the building of the railway. Much of the Argentine railway work was British led in terms of engineering, equipment and manpower. William Earsman was employed originally on the Bahia Blanca and North Western Railway, and while the work there was not about sheep, it was equally hard. William, it seems, went on to be a teacher.

The attraction was, however, mainly sheep. The sheep farming industry was the main economic base in Patagonia, and it was the most significant form of employment:

It is sheep and again sheep; sheep in the morning, sheep in the evening, sheep in the afternoon. And the Scot, like little Jack Horner, has his thumb in the pie, and has pulled out some plums.[1]

Caithness men – and their women – were drawn to Patagonia by the offer of sheep farming. Some of the men arrived, worked as shepherds and went home again. Others climbed the promotional ladder to become managers, and some established their own successful sheep farms, contributing to the development of Patagonia.

The rough tussock grass and the wide open spaces made Patagonian lands suitable for the rearing of sheep:

The pastoral capacity of the Patagonian scrub is on the average from 800 to 1200 head of sheep to 24 square kilometres. The ranch fixes the residence in the best part of the estate where there is least fear of a shortage of water and where pasture is most plentiful. To this the sheep are brought periodically to receive disinfecting baths against the scab and for shearing. These incessant movements toward the centre of the ranch cause an almost permanent strain on the pasture.[2]

In 21st-century Patagonia, the grasslands are in danger. Over the years the sheep have trampled the fields to the extent that the soil is loosened and the near-constant winds have blown much of the soil away. Some 20 million acres are now little more than blowing sand, and a major conservation project is in place to return this land to sheep rearing.[3]

Back in the late 19th century, any long-term impact was negated by immediate opportunity. By the time Caithnesian John Hamilton arrived with a small group of shepherds, who had learned their trade in the Falkland Islands, Patagonia was rapidly becoming the sheep capital of the world.

Sheep was an important aspect of Caithness farming, but the scale was different. A number of the Caithness Patagonian Pioneers came from shepherding families, and were to some extent familiar with sheep farming. This was especially true of the Earsman brothers, James and Percy; their father John Earsman came north from Scotland's Border counties to join the great sheep farming experiments in Sutherland.

Caithness and Sutherland provided a range of options for sheep grazing. The heather moors were able to carry fairly extensive quantities of sheep, and even some of the numerous Caithness peat bogs could support some levels of sheep farming. But nothing on a Patagonian scale.

In Patagonia, only some 40 or 50 years before the Caithness Pioneers arrived, sheep were of little significance. They were considered to be of little or no commercial value during the 1840s, their wool not worth the transportation costs. Mauricio Braun, the most significant of Patagonian sheep farmers, is known to have held on to wool for up to nine years before selling it, simply because the price was so low.

It was the governor of Punta Arenas, one Diego Duble Almeida, who showed an initiative to bring sheep across to Patagonia from the Falkland Islands, in 1876. While the ultimate success story owes much to John Hamilton and other Scottish pioneers, it was this Spaniard who foresaw the real business opportunity.

Despite the relative proximity between the Falkland Islands and the coast of Patagonia, the sheep had to endure a crossing which could take up to 20 days. Enough food (grass) as well as water was needed to ensure that the animals would stay healthy.[4] John Hamilton, who had cut his shepherding teeth in the Falklands, naturally considered the islands as a source for his stock; between 1878 and 1894 more than 20,000 sheep were brought over from the Falkland Islands to Punta Arenas[5] and to demonstrate the extent of the transfer of sheep farming business, '197 bank accounts were closed in Stanley'.[6] Interestingly, the Falkland Islands Company also recognised the potential of Patagonia, and attempted, but failed, to purchase land in Tierra del Fuego.

Various experiments were tried in terms of finding the best and most appropriate breeds of sheep for the Patagonian climate and lands. In 1884, Jose Menéndez bought his first 75,000 acres, and by 1896, he was expanding his 'empire', rearing millions of sheep and employing shepherds and managers. Cheviot sheep were among the first breeds farmed by Menéndez. Along with Mauricio Braun and Jose Nogueira, he was to establish such farms and own much of Patagonia. Nogueira acquired a million hectares of land on Tierra del Fuego and stocked it with sheep, cattle and horses. The Braun/ Menendez/Nogueira footprint owned much of the land, the banks, utility companies, insurance companies, shipping companies and refrigeration plants. The business was further cemented through marriage; Mauricio's sister Sara married Jose Nogueira, while Mauricio married Josefina Menéndez. By 1920 the empire had 1,250,000 sheep producing 5 million kilos of wool, and on average 2 million kilos of meat and offal.

The initial flocks of sheep came from the Falklands, but it quickly became evident there was a need to find a breed of sheep particularly suited to the Patagonian pampas. A number of breeds were crossed in an attempt to find the right mix of wool quality and quantity.

The Cheviot was the first breed to be introduced and it was crossed with the Falkland Island sheep. Large numbers of these crosses were imported into Patagonia, but they did not adapt well in most areas. Other breeds experimented with were Downs, Lincolns, Merino, Romney Marsh and Corriedale.

Where the soil was particularly good, the Cheviots fared well, producing wool of quality in quantity. However, in the springtime and after a bad winter when the grass was scarce, the Cheviot's wool root strand was found to have been weak. From about 1900 onwards fewer Cheviots were imported.

The Downs were never particularly successful. One report suggested that the black hairs on their legs ran up into their wool, leaving it of poorer quality. Lincoln rams were firstly introduced into the Rio Gallegas area from England; these rams were used extensively for crossbreeding, and as a result the true breed effectively disappeared. The resulting crossbreeds did, however, produce thick wool – but unfortunately their heavy wool coats put them in danger during severe winters; the frost and snow became enmeshed in the thick wool, leaving the sheep unable to move freely and consequently suffer in the cold.[7]

The Romney Marsh breed was hardy and suited the Patagonian conditions. These sheep had the ability to withstand the cold and to exist on an often sparse diet. They were good producers of both wool and meat, and therefore were favoured by many sheep farmers. Corriedales, first introduced into Patagonia around 1905, became one of the main Patagonian breeds. They were crossbred Merino and Lincoln, and had the advantage of high quality wool and meat. They were also blessed with a relatively lengthy life span.[8]

Merinos became fairly widespread about 1898, when they were introduced from New Zealand. The Merino is, of course, prized for its wool. As an excellent forager, it is well suited to many parts of Patagonia. Today, Estancia Morro Chico, one of John Hamilton's original sheep farms, produces top grade Merino wool, used by the Patagonia Clothing Company:

At Estancia Morro Chico (Little Hill Farm), John Hamilton's great-grandson, Stephen Gallie, runs 13,000 sheep and 1,800 head of cattle on one of the farms founded by his great-grandfather. His 64,000-acre estancia at the foot of the southern Andes still supports a healthy population of native grasses. But Stephen says productivity is declining and an invasive weed is beginning to take root because of overgrazing.[9]

In an initial attempt to stock their southern Patagonian farms, John Hamilton, Thomas Saunders, Henry Jamieson, John McLean and George McGeorge[10] embarked on the now legendary two-year trek, herding a vast quantity of sheep and horses some 2,000 miles across Argentina from Neocochea to Rio Gallegos. First taking a boat to Buenos Aires via Montevideo and then a train to Bahia Blanca, they reached the starting point for their trek. Here they acquired 200 horses and 400 mares, and having recruited native guides, set off for Rio Negro, to gather some 5,000 sheep, mainly crossbred Merinos. On 18 September 1888, they set off with the sheep.

Tiredness was one of the main challenges for the sheep, but the lack of water was to prove a critical element in their survival. The herding party followed Indian trails to try and ensure that sheep, horses and men could access whatever water was available. Local guides were used where possible, but they were not always reliable. Thomas Saunders, in a diary he kept during the journey, records his frustration in an entry dated 27 February 1889: 'Started again and came about 5 leagues and stopped, as the guide is a thick-head and cannot remember where the cut-off is: has to go and look for tracks.'[11]

A chance meeting during the drive between John Hamilton and a scientist named Burmeister helped pinpoint likely water sources. However, where fresh water was found there was also the danger of finding pumas. On at least one occasion they woke in the morning to find the effects of a puma visit; dead sheep were scattered around. Ingenuity was vital to their success and survival. On reaching the Rio Deseado River, where it proved impossible to get the sheep across, they constructed a bridge out of bushes, grass turf and guanaco skin.

The sheep slowly developed a sense of direction. At first they seemed to want to go in a northwards direction, but as time went on, they began to understand that the direction should be southerly.

The first winter the trek team spent at San Julián, where fellow Scot Donald Munro had already established himself as a sheep farmer, albeit still apparently living in a tent. San Julián had been first colonised around 1780 by a group sent from Buenos Aires to commence populating the region, although this initial settlement lasted only until 1784, when it was abandoned on the orders of Buenos Aires. San Julián has a natural harbour, making it an important location for the export of wool. In the late 1870s Swift & Co. also saw its potential, and established a refrigeration plant just north of the town.

The staple diet on the trek was guanaco and ostrich, with the occasional wether[12] for a change. On one occasion, John Hamilton spotted a herd of cattle in the distance.

The party ate well for a few days once some of the bullocks in the herd had been rounded up and killed.

Sheep died and lambs were born *en route*. Where and when the herders could, they sheared the sheep and sold the wool to local merchants. This was to be an important source of money during the journey. At the end of the journey, each of the partners ended up with around 2,000 sheep. The journey these pioneers made is now legendary – not just because of its magnitude, but because of the relative inexperience of the five leading shepherds: 'The track behind them was white with bones and black with vultures.'[13]

Ultimately, vast quantities of sheep roamed the estancia lands. The rams were put to the ewes between May and June, with subsequent lambing taking place out in the camp[14] during September and October. The lambs remained with their mothers for around four months, before being separated and marked on their ears and also having their tails docked.

Farmers calculated the success of the lambing by the tally of tails that they had cut off the new lambs; their tails were cut down to a stump to prevent the wool getting contaminated by faeces and urine, attracting the blowfly maggots that would eat the sheep alive. Then one ear was marked with the year, and the other with the mark of the estancia. The sheep were usually allowed to lamb four or five times before being sent to the slaughterhouse. A future balance between male and female sheep was achieved by castrating an appropriate number of male lambs.

Keeping the sheep healthy was imperative. While gauchos patrolled the vast sheep lands, the sheep might be a long way away from the estancia. The sheep would be rounded up and brought back to the estancia two or three times a year. They were usually dipped twice or three times a year to prevent them from getting scab, maggots and other parasitical diseases. Obviously the number of sheep dipped each time varied according to stock size but, as with all other estancia tasks, action was paramount. Estancia Laguna Colorado was situated approximately 10 miles from Rio Gallegas and covered an area of 6 leagues[15] and housed 9,000 sheep;[16] it took the men two days to dip 4,200 ewes.[17]

The development that led to sheep dip being standardised, packaged and transportable in quantity was critical for the Patagonian 'industrial scale' sheep farming, where thousands of sheep had to be thus treated. Traditional methodologies that had involved the smearing of sheep with tar and goose grease was not a realistic method for Patagonian sheep farmers. William Cooper's introduction in England of Cooper's Sheep Dip enabled sheep farmers to immerse the sheep in a trough instead of the previous laborious method. The whole of the sheep could now be evenly treated.

While Coopers became a major player in the market, Scotland lays claim to the original sheep dip. George Wilson of Coldstream reputedly invented sheep dip in the 1830s; it was manufactured in the town and then transported by horse and cart to the port of Berwick for export across the world. The Oban-based form of Robertson's sheep dip also operated in the Patagonia sheep dip market, although Robertsons was later amalgamated with Coopers into the firm of Cooper, MacDougall and Robertson.

Late January or early February would see the first dipping, followed in early May and then again in August.[18] Originally the Patagonian dip was made of wood and was up to 25 metres long; Robert Nicolson and George Bain had arrived in Patagonia from Caithness with the necessary woodworking skills to construct wooden sheep dips of around 20 metres in length. In the early years of the 20th century, sheep dips began to be constructed from cement, and held 35,000 litres of water. The sheep would remain in the tank for about a minute while their heads were submerged a few times.

An example of the early wooden dips can be seen at the now largely deserted Estancia San Gregoria, once one of the biggest and most significant estancias in Patagonia. This farm was almost 220,000 acres or 360 square miles[19] and held 123,000 sheep and 4,000 horses.

The outputs from sheep farming are meat and wool. Up to 5,000 sheep or more might be sheared in one day. The work was hard and the hours were long. Shepherds would begin their work at about 3 a.m. in order to be able to round up the sheep and have them back at the shearing sheds before the heat of the midday sun. The shearing sheds, however, were places of much activity and camaraderie.

Shearing would begin between October and January, when teams of shearers would arrive – a situation that continues today – but the conditions in the early Patagonian days were pretty basic. Seven shillings per 100 sheep sheared was a figure quoted during the later years of the 19th century. A good shearer could shear up to 140 sheep in a day, all done by hand until mechanised equipment arrived:

> The shearing machines vary in number from five to 30, according to the size of the estancia and are driven by a propeller shaft, driven in turn by a steam engine. The movement is transmitted to the rod by an articulated shearing machine in two parts, each joint having a gear and the latter has two cutting combs. Each Shearer finds an animal, takes it in his arms and carries and sits on the sheep's hindquarters, placing it between his legs. The worker works standing, his body bent; clipper held with one hand and holding the animal with the other; begins his work by the belly, followed by members and the sides and ends of the back, so that the fleece out of one piece.[20]

William Hendry from Caithness was at one time employed at Estancia Rincon los Morros, which was located near the Chilean–Argentine border. This estancia extended over nine miles and was by Patagonian standards one of the most modern in terms of equipment. Its shearing shed had eight hydraulic press scissors, and the estancia employed 20 labourers. Each shearing team brought with it its own cook. He would select a suitable sheep, and that would be lunch for the shearers.

Once the wool was away from the sheep any belly wool would be removed from the fleece, and the fleeces wrapped into bales of about 200 kg. However, because of the amount of dust that gathered in the fleece, the wool once cleaned could weigh up to half as much as when it was initially removed from the sheep. (Stephen Gallie at Estancia Morro Chico continues to deliberately shear by hand, with the aim of leaving a thin layer of wool on the sheep to help protect them from the cold.)

In order to get the fleeces to market, the bales of wool had to be transported to the nearest port for shipment. Most of the towns on the coast served as points of collection. In the early days, it was not always possible to predict when a ship would arrive, so the wool would be stacked in bales on the beach, covered with a tarpaulin and left there until a boat arrived. Each farmer would have his signature attached to his bundle of bales.

Convoys of carts, pulled by teams of oxen or mules and piled high with wool bales would be seen travelling to Rio Gallegas and the other coastal towns. The carts weighed in the region of three tons and carried a load of five tons. The cartwheels were very large, raising the carts to a height that enabled them to manoeuvre over the rough tracks, and high enough to enable the carters to sleep underneath them overnight. Estancia San Gregoria, one of the largest of the farms, had a railway system built to transport its wool to the port.

Patagonia was a growing region, important in economic terms for Argentina, and a vital source of meat and wool for a worldwide market. Santa Cruz province annually produced around 20 million kilos of wool. Originally most of the wool and mutton was shipped directly to Europe, and Britain in particular, until the Argentine government began to realise its internal economic potential.

In the latter years of the 1890s Argentina attempted to build up its own fleet of ships, designed to travel around the coast collecting the wool and mutton for the home market. This initial attempt at cornering the market proved less than successful, as companies could or would not commit the capital. Eventually with government intervention and support, a shipping service along the Argentine coast was established. By the early 1900s, the expanding Braun Menendez empire also moved into the world of shipping.

Today Argentina remains one of the top producers of wool, although at the end of the First World War there was a significant drop in price. This was mainly due to a fall-off in demand for military uniforms. The result was bankruptcy for some businesses, as the selling prices did not even cover costs.

1 *Padre in Patagonia* – http://www.electricscotland.com/history/argentina/lecture2.htm
2 *The Argentine Republic: Its Development and Progress*/ Pierre Denis. 1922.
3 Shear Salvation/ Julian Smith in *Nature* magazine.
4 *Malvinas and Santa Cruz: a historical relationship broken by war*/ Maria de los Milagros and Pablo Gustavo Beecher.

5   The Pioneer Farmers of Patagonia in *Falklands Island Journal* 1981 p. 10.

6   *FIC's Aborted Project of Sheep Ranching in Patagonia*/ Fernando Coronato.

7   Short History of the Territories Live Stock in *Patagonia Argentina*.

8   The livestock in the region of the southern highlands of Santa Cruz territory.1917.

9   http://www.patagonia.com/eu/enGB/patagonia.go?assetid=100810.

10   *From the Falklands to Patagonia*/ Michael James Mainwaring. Alison & Busby. 1983.

11   *Diary of a sheep-drive from the Río Negro to San Julián*/ Thomas Saunders, September 1888–March 1889.

12   Castrated male sheep.

13   *Life & Work*: the magazine of the Church of Scotland. 1925.

14   The countryside.

15   A league as a unit of area (as against length) was a traditional Spanish measure equivalent to approx. 4 acres or 1.8 hectares.

16   http://patlibros.org/lpa/vwran/laguna-colorada.htm.

17   http://www.patbrit.org/eng/events/rr1920pocock.htm.

18   Cómo se trabaja en las estancias patagónicas – http://patlibros.org/lpa/vwoth/como-se-trabaja.htm.

19   *Railways of the Far South* http://www.railwaysofthefarsouth.co.uk.

20   El Ganado Lanar: descripción publicada por el Instituto Comercial de Punta Arenas, 1944.

Meat

Patagonian towns grew to accommodate the needs of the population and the infrastructure of the sheep farming industry. Increasing quantities of meat products for shipment, combined with the unreliability of shipping, fuelled the drive to build refrigeration plants; fierce and volatile weather made it difficult for ships to stick to schedules, and without refrigeration sheep carcasses could not wait. The town of Puerto Santa Cruz, for example, in 1890 had 'about six houses'. But by 1919 it had grown significantly and could boast:

> *four big Stores and other shops: three Butchers, two Bakers, two Shoe Makers, one Watch Maker and other business Houses. There is one skating ring [sic], two Cinematographs; they have a Club of Spanish & English mixed. We have Mail Boats coming every month from Buenos Aires.*[1]

The necessity for building freezer plants was realised early; within a period of some ten years from the early 1900s, ten freezing plants were established throughout Patagonia. The vast quantities of sheep, the distance to ports for export and the uncertainty and infrequency of shipping meant that some form of local production and storage was necessary:

> *They froze old wedders at first, then they began to try yearlings, which weigh about 56lbs, and now they have begun to kill them as lambs.*[2]

Refrigeration plants were established at the main ports, although there seems to have been some government resistance in Chile. The southern and eastern Patagonian estancias would send their sheep to Rio Gallegas, Puerto San Julián, Puerto Santa Cruz or Puerto Deseado. Those in the more western regions naturally favoured the Chilean plants such as Puerto Bories.

The Puerto Deseado Frigorifico was built in the late 1920s by one of the Braun companies, and was operated by CAP (Corporación Argentina de Productores de Carne). Sheep would arrive by train and be sorted and counted before moving through to the slaughterhouse. The main function at this plant was to produce frozen mutton for export.

David Barnetson from Caithness gained employment at the CAP Deseado plant. His application for the post of sheep counter was supported and endorsed by his fellow Caithnesian, Angus Robert Bain. Puerto Deseado is now a major fishing port for prawns, and the frigorifico is used as a freezer plant for the seafood.[3]

In 1914, the refrigeration plant Frigorifico Bories was opened at Última Esperanza (Last Hope), with a capacity of processing 500,000 sheep annually.[4] The plant and much of the sheep farming land in the region was owned by Sociedad Explotadora de Tierra del Fuego, a multinational alliance of those who dominated sheep farming in the southern Patagonian region. Massive numbers of sheep were processed in these meat processing plants; Frigorifico Bories slaughtered the following numbers of animals:

- 1918   301,659
- 1919   5,698
- 1920   213,855
- 1921   279,020
- 1922   261,278
- 1923   350,326.[5]

The relatively small number in 1919 can be explained by the fact that this was the year of the workers' revolution at the plant.

Swift & Company was the main operator of the refrigeration plants on the eastern ports. Here too, vast numbers of sheep were being slaughtered; in 1916 it produced figures showing a total of 280,000 carcasses.

The Frigorifico Bories Refrigeration Plant was more than just a slaughterhouse. It was a significant factory, with all parts of the sheep being prepared for the market. The carcasses were placed in cold stores, awaiting shipment. The cold store could hold 850,000 tons of meat.

The hearts, kidneys and other edible parts were removed and processed as canned meat, with cooking and canning processes also taking place on the site. Most of the chilled mutton was shipped to Europe. The wool was also, of course, washed, dried and baled for shipment.

The refrigeration plants also required infrastructure and machinery commensurate with these levels of operation. The efficient working of the motors was crucial to ensuring the plant ran smoothly. Frigorifico Bories installed two motors, British made, in case one should break down. A system of small railway lines was constructed to transport the carcasses around the various process stages. In the case of Frigorifico Bories, the rail tracks extended out onto a jetty; its wagons could then reach the ships waiting to transport the mutton to market. The plants were designed to have the animals arrive on their own feet before being transported around the processes and finally loaded onto the relatively small ships that could access the small jetties.

If the animals were to arrive 'on their own feet' they had to be driven from the estancias. Estancia Morro Chico, for example, was a significant distance from Rio Gallegas and with large numbers of sheep it could take up to 17 days for the animals to reach their destination. Caithness Patagonian pioneer Alexander Plowman was a manager at Estancia Stag River, and would have been on these long treks. To help facilitate the sheep drives, the Swift and Company arranged for pens to be set up at various points along the route.[6] Around 3,000 sheep could have been accumulated outside the plant before being divided up and despatched into the slaughterhouse.

While sheep was the main business, the facilities were also brought into use when whales had been caught or washed ashore.

The refrigeration plants were, by necessity, often some distance away from the actual town. Access to a suitable harbour and an extensive piece of land was required. Special workers' barracks were constructed, either onsite or, as at Frigorifico Bories, at a distance that necessitated a train to run between the plant and the 'company' town of Puerto Bories, making regular trips to and from the workers' homes.

Transportation to the dockside plants demanded improved road infrastructure, and British expertise was sought. In 1909 J. H. & W Bell, a firm of builders from Liverpool, was contracted to build a two-mile length of road that included a bridge over the River Gallegos. The local area had next to no trees for the necessary timber, so along with a gang of workmen came a shipload of timber, pneumatic riveting machines, cranes and pumps.[7]

Not all refrigeration plants were on such a huge scale. Caithness Patagonian James Earsman bought a farm near Puerto Natales, and also established a slaughterhouse and a butchery for the local village. He was obviously something of a community person, as he also established a social club in Puerto Natales with the aim of bringing people together.

---

1 Letter from Puerto Santa Cruz (1919) by Mrs Mary Ellen Betts. http://www.patbrit.org/eng/events/rr-1919betts.htm.
2 *The Scotsman* 2 April 1909.
3 *Railways of the Far South* http://www.railwaysofthefarsouth.co.uk
4 *The Scotsman* 10 July 1914.
5 Álbum Última Esperanza http://patlibros.org/aue/.
6 http://patbrit.org/eng/events/granarreo.htm
7 *Daily Mail* 9 October 1909.

A Working Life

For the men and women from Caithness who crossed the Atlantic to this far and foreign shore in response to a shepherding opportunity, life was hard and the existence meagre. The Patagonian shepherd spent many a day alone with his horse and dog, and slept out in all weathers. To be a Patagonian shepherd you needed to have a special character with extraordinary physical and mental strength. The Patagonian shepherd was a key member of a successful sheep farm, and it was generally accepted that the best Patagonian shepherds were either Scottish or Australian.

The shepherds of Patagonia would spend much of their time alone and on horseback, often miles from any real human contact. Allegedly, on arrival in Patagonia the pioneer would be provided with a horse, given a day to become familiar with it, and would set off to the camp the next day. He would spend many days on horseback traversing the fields, where his tasks were numerous. Fences had to be checked and repaired, sheep needed help lambing, and when the sheep were sick they had to be cared for. Unfortunately, it also fell to the shepherd to destroy the bodies of the sheep that did not survive. As they were destined to work and live in far-flung and isolated estancias, their supplies had to be shipped from the towns, maybe only once or twice a year, with payment often being held on credit until the wool was sold.

In Caithness, horsemanship had related more to the working horses that pulled the ploughs and the carts. So the horses and the horsemanship encountered in Patagonia must have been at first something quite alien. John Hamilton is reputed to have 'had a way' with horses, and Angus MacPherson dealt in horses, or at least had shares in a company that dealt in horses. Angus was indeed an expert horseman, taking part in polo and show jumping events. William Cormack, son of Caithness Patagonian pioneer John Cormack, was also an excellent horse tamer. The Patagonian shepherd's job was not without its challenges, and there were many broken and bruised bones resulting from falls; William Begg is thought to have met his death after being thrown from a horse.

The shepherds, when away for long periods, would normally have a number of horses with them. Long distances had to be covered, so spare horses were a necessity. But the horses themselves presented a persistent problem by frequently going missing; to all intents and purposes, they were wild horses that had been tamed to some extent. Tying up one horse last thing at night so that it could be used to help find the deserting horses was common practice.

The horses used by sheep farmers in Patagonia were originally wild or used by the native tribes. The Tehuelche tribe were recognised horse breakers, and one of the Tehuelche, Capipe, was employed by John Hamilton to rebreak horses that had been badly broken.[1] Capipe worked on the Hamilton Estancia at Punta Loyola, and was held in high esteem by John Hamilton.

The Patagonian shepherd was extremely reliant on his dogs. A single shepherd on horseback could have responsibility for between 1,000 and 2,000 sheep. Given the huge distances involved, herding such numbers would have been impossible without well-bred and well-trained dogs. A preferred breed of dog was the Scottish collie, and a shepherd might have up to ten dogs. Mauricio Braun, the sheep-farming entrepreneur, is reputed to have brought some 300 border collies to Patagonia. Patagonia also has its own 'Lassie' story, commemorated by a statue of the gaucho and his dog; the legend tells of how the gaucho fell from his horse and broke a leg. Unable to get back onto his horse, he tied his neck scarf to the dog, which took a day to get home and bring back help.

Many of the early Caithness Patagonian settlers began life as little more than squatters. At best the shepherds were provided with a shack to live in. Basic in the extreme, it would consist of a small stove, a bed, a table and chair. At certain times, of course, more communal activities were necessary. Then the scenes around the farms and towns of Patagonia would be one of 'men working like ants'.

Before any form of social relaxation could be considered, the priority was to eat and sleep in preparation for the next day's work. In fact, for some the working day was governed by what became known as 'estancia time'; in order to ensure that the workers did a significant amount of toil before their midday break, some farmers were known to deliberately re-adjust the clocks.

A custom in Sutherland and in other parts of the north of Scotland was for shepherds to be allowed to keep a small number, or 'pack', of sheep, as part of their wages. In Scotland, the pack was an agreed number of sheep plus a couple of cows, which were the property of the shepherd, not the flock master. They would be herded with the main flock and the proceeds from the sale of any lambs and wool produced went to the shepherd. Patrick Sellar, the infamous Sutherland flock master, explained what he gave each of his shepherds.[2]

A cottage, a garden, 13 bolls of meal, grass for three cows and a pony, with the profits to be derived from seventy Cheviot sheep of the different sorts, each mixed with the master's sheep of the same kind.[3]

In Patagonia it was also fairly common for shepherds to acquire sheep of their own and by this means potentially build up their own flocks. Caithness Patagonian pioneer John Cormack seems to have started his own farm in this way.

The Patagonian weather ate into the soul, and the living conditions provided little in the way of relief. For those thinking of making the journey, Greta Mackenzie's father had this advice:

Here's a word to boys at home
If you want to roam
Don't come to Patagonia
This God-forsaken shore
The only time you're happy here
Is when you are asleep.
For when you wake,
You are tormented
By dogs and scabby sheep.[4]

There are numerous tales of the Patagonian winters, with the disastrous impact the snow had on the flocks of sheep. Caithness is no stranger to a mix of weather conditions, and throughout the years violent snowstorms have impacted on farming. In 1880, Caithness suffered a particularly heavy snowfall with a significant loss of sheep – but it is the scale that is the difference, and nothing would have prepared for Patagonian winters:

To the Patagonian sheep breeder a 'bad' winter – a heavy layer of snow, which for months refuses to melt – means hard times for all. For the manager, overseer, shepherd and peon – literally all hands but the cook – it entails gruelling rescue work, while to the flocks of suffering sheep it brings growing, freezing misery and the dread menace of a lingering death from exhaustion and starvation.

A 'bad' winter, say 1899 or 1904, when starving horses denuded one another of every vestige of hair, from mane to tail, there being nothing to eat … The sheep also consumed every particle of their fellow sufferer›s fleeces, some died frozen stiff in an upright position and when the snow ultimately cleared away, the highest trees were festooned with the carcasses of animals which had browsed off the tree tops.[5]

Sheep will crowd for shelter into a bush. Then the snow will come and completely bury both sheep and bush. The warmth of the animals' bodies will melt the snow, which will reform around them in an insurmountable ring of ice. The sheep will eat the bush, gnawing the wood down to the roots, and then starve.[6]

On a somewhat lighter note is the story of how a consignment of turkeys was left in a tree overnight and in the morning were all hanging upside down, having frozen overnight. There is also the account given of the gaucho who, when caught in a fierce snowstorm with no shelter and no hope of finding anywhere, killed the horse, gutted it and then lived inside the horse's ribcage for some days until the weather cleared.[7]

Because not every Patagonian winter is bad, there was a tendency to leave sheep out during the mild winters. But experience showed that those sheep were in danger of becoming acclimatised to warmer, milder winters and were as a consequence very vulnerable when a bad snow did arrive. The one positive regarding the snow was that it provided some welcome moisture to the normally dry lands. As spring took hold in Patagonia, the sheep began to grow as the vegetation began to sprout. The tasks of the shepherd also began to expand. Lambing time brings with it the need for closer attention; some sheep, still weak after a hard winter, would need help.

1912 was a bad winter for Robert Nicolson on Estancia Koluel Kike. In a letter home to his brother he shared the extent of the problem:

Koluel Kaike marked 3,000 lambs and shore 20,000 Kilos of wool, less than last year. I only marked 800 lambs and shore more or less the same quantity of wool as last year.[8]

Things were only marginally better the next year. Donald Nicolson at Estancia Hercules had marked about 4,000 lambs, while his brother Robert had marked only 600. Donald Bain managed to mark 3,500. Nevertheless a sum of $10 per kilo was expected for wool. Again, in 1914 Robert Nicolson returned to Patagonia from Caithness, only to find that due to heavy snowfall many of his sheep had been lost.

For a life that was naturally centred outdoors, the winter months could completely shut everything down. Motorised transport, where it existed, was no longer viable when the snow was lying many feet deep. It could become so cold that indoors the water in the jugs would freeze. Horseback was the only possible means of looking after the sheep out on the camp; pieces of animal hides would be tied around the horse's legs to protect them from ice.

It was not just the winters, of course that were challenging. While the snow lay deep in the winter months, the summer months would be marked by an incessant wind. The winds in some parts can achieve around 125 miles per hour and blow for days. So strong are the winds that they can knock over everything, from cars to cattle; someone once said that Patagonia without the wind would be like hell without the devil.

The direction, frequency and intensity of winds largely defines the characteristics of the regional climate, which affects the development of soils, vegetation distribution and modelling of landscapes.[9]

Caithness was rarely dry enough for its inhabitants to worry about drought. But the Patagonian pampa, as we have seen, was not only vast but also arid. Farmers would use traditional Y-shaped divining rods to find water sources; wells were dug and windmills were erected to pump water supplies for the sheep.

New skills needed to be learned for a working life in Patagonia. The necessity of catching animals such as the guanaco for food and clothing was one particular skill new to the Caithness Patagonian Pioneers. Caithness people were not without the skills of hunting; from rabbits to deer, legitimately or not, these were fair game. Traps and guns were the Caithness hunting weapons – but in Patagonia they found a new tool.

The native population had perfected the art of the *boleadoras* or bolas. It consists of stone balls tied together and wrapped in a strip of twisted hide. The boleadoras is held by one of the balls and whirled around the thrower's head before being launched towards the intended prey. The intention is to get the balls to wrap around the animal's legs, thereby bringing it down and making it unable to move. Experts could achieve a good strike rate from as far away as 50 yards or more.[10] The native Tehuelche tribe had three types of bolas: one with three balls that was used in hunting guanaco; one with two balls which was for hunting ostriches; and one with just the one ball which they used when fighting or attacking other humans.

1 *The British in Santa Cruz territory* 1911–2011/ María de los Milagros Pierini and Pablo Gustavo Beecher. Edición del Club Británico de Río Gallegos
2 *Two Hundred Years of Farming in Sutherland*/ Reay D G Clarke.
3 *Farm Reports 3 County of Sutherland*/ Patrick Sellar.
4 *Return to Patagonia*/ Greta Mackenzie. Islands Book Trust 2011.
5 Bad Winters in Patagonia/ by Calafate – *Blackwood's Magazine,* April 1935.
6 *The Outermost Parts of the Earth*/ E Lucas Bridges. 1947.
7 As re-told by Donald MacDonald.
8 http://www.patbrit.org/eng/events/rr1912nicolson.htm.
9 *La Provincia de Santa Cruz*/ Mazzoni and Vazquez, 2000: 5.
10 *The Way Southward*/ A. F. Tschiffely. 1945.

A New Home

Patagonia was a land that greeted our Caithness Pioneers, and in many cases made them the men they became. Their resilience meant that many built up successful businesses and families, and while some preferred to return home, Patagonia today continues to be a testament to, and remembers, the contributions made by the many Scots, including those from Caithness.

The Caithness men and women who made their homes near, or visited, the coastal areas would have recognised one bird – the 'scorrie'; seagulls, with their natural talent for scavenging, were regular visitors to the freezer plants.

Loneliness must have been one of the main challenges faced by the earliest Patagonian shepherds. On horseback they would have spent long hours and sometimes days traversing the wide and barren landscapes, only to return home to an isolated hut:

When he rides home from the campo at dusk – the wind biting … there is no soul in the vicinity to share his meal. He opens the door to the tiny indoor world and creeps into a silent grey room.[1]

There is a theory that people who are alone for long periods become almost hermit-like and begin to shun the company of others. They lose the ability to communicate and empathise with others. On the other hand, being alone offers time for thinking. As W. H. Hudson wrote, following his Patagonian journey:

To my mind there is nothing in life as delightful as that feeling of relief, of escape and absolute freedom which one experiences in vast solitude.[2]

A poignant account of the initial conditions experienced in Patagonia comes from the diaries of Caithness emigrant and shepherd Angus MacPherson. In January 1901 he records his despondency and loneliness for there are: 'no Britishers to talk to and nothing to read'.

The Caithness brothers Angus and Hugh MacPherson were employed on the vast Braun lands of Última Esperanza. Later, Angus built a significant house for his mother in Halkirk, Caithness, and in memory of their time in Patagonia at Rio

Guillermo named it 'Esperanza'. It is a far cry from the log house the brothers had built with only an axe and a saw.

Life had not improved for Angus by 1903 when on 4 July he wrote:

> *Today is a great day in North America and I would like to be in New York today. How strange is human nature? Today I am sick of this country or at least the weary lonesome life, which we lead here, the same dreary job over and over again without even a woman's smile to help us along day after day. If I could sell my animals I would clear out right away to South Africa or Canada. I will never bring myself to like this part of the world. Let me live in a country where there is some life. It's as well to be in a prison as here. Tomorrow I may feel quite different, I think there is a storm gathering.*

This from a man who some ten years later *did* sell up and move to Canada, only to return again to Patagonia.

Enough to drive you mad! The Rev. Douglas Bruce, a minister in Patagonia during the early 1920s, recounts the tale of a shepherd who was brought into the town of Rio Gallegas from the foothill of the Andes, 'quite loco'. He refused to eat for days until presented with some tinned herring, which seemed to bring back some memories of his days as a fisherman on the coast of Scotland. More personal comforts in terms of female companionship were also, naturally, sought; George Blain, from the Scottish Borders, whose diaries are now in the National Archive of Scotland, wrote: 'The boss wants to know when I am going to get a Squaw – to make the beds!'[3]

In general, close relationships between the pioneers and the native women were discouraged by both the immigrant population and the native tribes. In reality it was more likely that mixed-race people would be found living among the tribes than on the estancias. Generally people married someone they either knew or who came from their own cultural origins. The original Caithness Pioneers, by and large, married within their social and ethnic group.

Regular trips home to the family halfway across the world meant that contact was not lost, and no doubt provided the reassurance needed to set off again. We can see from various records that many of the pioneers married into other pioneer families. A number of the Caithness Patagonian Pioneers journeyed back to Caithness to marry Caithness women. Caithness men were consequently being joined by Caithness women in opening up this new land.

The Bain brothers all returned to Caithness to find their wives, as did Alexander Nicol, John Cormack, Hugh McPherson, Henry Christian and John MacKinnon. Nicol Oman returned to Inverness to marry. Donald MacKay, son of Caithness pioneer James MacKay, despite being born in Patagonia, found his wife on a trip to Caithness. James, himself was married in Caithness before departing for Patagonia.

Benn Cormack also married a Caithness girl prior to leaving Caithness. Angus McPherson married in Canada before returning with his wife to Patagonia. Percy Earsman married into a Sutherland family, originally from Brora, near the Caithness border. Meanwhile, the two Bain sisters, already in Patagonia, married Scotsmen there. William Begg, John Hamilton, John Harper and Alexander Plowman all married British girls already in Patagonia. Alexander Nicolson married another member of the extended Bain family. John Munro married a lady of Swedish origin. David Barnetson and Robert MacDonald were the exceptions as they married ladies of Argentine/Spanish descent – Maria Cozzetti and Fernanda Garcia respectively.

Caithness women were also setting out on their own adventure into the unknown. Theoretically these pioneering wives would, one hopes, have been given some indication by their prospective husbands of what awaited them in Patagonia. Nevertheless they needed all of their Caithnesian hardiness, as they too were confronted with a life of relative isolation and danger.

As John McKinnon's wife Williamina discovered, one of the first lessons some of the women learned was how to handle a rifle. Left alone, while husbands were away for days, the women had to see to it not just that the rifle above the fireplace was ready and primed, but also that when pumas or hostile natives came calling they themselves were ready to use it effectively. There are a number of anecdotal accounts of the native people taking an opportunity when the men were away to capture and spirit away women and children.

Few, if any, of these Caithness ladies would have needed these shooting skills on their Caithness crofts. Women would have had limited experience of firearms, but many men from Caithness would have used rifles on their farms to shoot rabbits and other vermin. Plus there is a long history of rifle shooting clubs in the county.

While the men were the ones who worked and developed the sheep farming industry of Patagonia, it was the women who very often were left to hold together the home and the family. While their existence on some of the remote estancias was in many ways a million miles away from their lives back in Britain, there was a strong similarity in that women on the crofts of Caithness also had to shoulder the burden of being largely homebound.

To the women fell the task of maintaining a house and home wherever they lived, but circumstances and conditions in Patagonia added experiences that from even their upbringing in remote Caithness they could never have imagined. In some ways their new lives also mirrored the lives of the women of the native Patagonian tribes. They too had the task of cooking and raising the family, plus the additional one of carrying the tribe's tents and equipment as they moved location.

Beyond mutton, fruit and vegetables from the estancia garden were the basic ingredients for home cooking. Sometimes the diet could be supplemented with a fresh trout from the river. John Cormack's children remember their mother Annie (née Chapman) being a proficient seamstress, sewing and making new clothes, all made on the farm. At one point a Singer sewing machine was ordered from Europe, and this must have made life considerably easier for her. She of course passed her sewing and knitting skills on to the rest of the family.[4]

Annie Chapman, born 1883 in Upper Lybster, married Caithness Patagonian pioneer John Cormack in Glasgow in 1905. At the time of her marriage, Annie was a dressmaker – a far cry from the wife of a Patagonian farmer. Once in Patagonia she found herself keeping a pig for slaughtering around April or May and producing hams and sausages.

For milk the Cormack family kept a few cows. Cattle were never suited to eastern Patagonian conditions, especially on any kind of farming scale. Those that did exist were kept mainly to supply milk. As you move into more western areas of Patagonia, where the grass is greener, significant herds of cattle are now farmed; John Hamilton's great grandson keeps some 1,500 head of Hereford cattle on Estancia Morro Chico.

Life for many of these early pioneers did improve. Despite the fact that conditions were difficult, they were earning wages. A keenness on the part of the authorities to sell plots of land enabled many of our Caithness Pioneers to establish their own estancias. The government in Buenos Aires decided that the lands of Patagonia were only fit for sheep farming, so in 1882 a law was passed that made the acquisition of land in the territory possible at low cost. The maximum amount of land that could be acquired under this law was 40,000 hectares (approximately 100,000 acres or 153 square miles, an area of 12 × 12 miles), which meant that those with the most money could begin to acquire large areas of Patagonia.

By 1893 it was estimated that the Argentine government had assigned around 2,500,000 hectares (about 10,000 square miles) of Santa Cruz to only 40 landowners.[5] Those who did not follow the ownership route found that their skills and abilities often translated into promotion to manager status.

Land ownership has always been a key element in a Scotsman's life. Especially those from the Caithness parishes of Latheron and Halkirk, who still bore the scars of the Highland Clearances. To them, the collective memories of their communities retained stories of land rights and disputes. Even by the time the first of the Caithness Patagonian Pioneers were departing, land ownership and tenant rights were still very much part of their everyday lives. For example, tenants on the Clyth Estate, which was owned by a Mr Sharp, protested at unfair rent rises. In true Caithness style the matter was considered and debated before acting.

The action however was decisive:

> Instead of coming to pay, the farmers appeared before the landlord, Mr Sharp, and demanded a revaluation and an abatement. This was refused, and the tenants immediately betook themselves to a large field, where they held a meeting, at which some bold words were uttered. John Sinclair said that 'if Mr Sharp got the law to protect him they must resist the law as far as possible till they got redress' John Forbes remarked that 'twenty years of oppression had brought them there that day;

they must not go back or look back, though at the same time they must take care not to act as criminals'.

Donald Grant proposed that 'the House divide' – those willing to pay rent to take the left, and those not willing to pay to take the right. Every man present marched to the right.[6]

The Patagonian estancias were huge in terms of acreage. In Scotland a farm of 1,000 acres would be considered significant – but in Patagonia it was not unusual in the early days to find a sheep farm of 270,000 acres. The many pioneers who left small Caithness farms and crofts must have found this agricultural vastness bewildering – and we can only imagine the reaction of those who came from a life in town like Wick, even though it served as an urban centre for a very rural hinterland. John Hamilton, son of a clothier, Alexander Nicol, son of a hotelkeeper, and John Harper, son of a shoemaker, must have been utterly taken aback by this rural vastness. Even today, Patagonia's magnitude creates a sense of amazement.

Originally settlers and incoming farmers had little restriction as to the size of their lands. Later the Argentine government was to place a restriction of a maximum of 40,000 acres per farm. This inevitably led to the breakup of some of the larger farms, but it did enable many who were previously managers to become farmers in their own right.

The estancias were of course businesses, and had to be run as such. Estancias consisted of a variety of buildings and areas. Houses were required for the owner, the manager and the workers. Also essential were sheep dips, corrals for horses, shearing sheds and crucially a wind-powered water pump. To run this setup, a number of employees were necessary.

For example a typical Patagonian farm would have a foreman, a foreman shepherd, and a number of shepherds and labourers. The labourers were known as *peons*, and were given whatever task needed doing. In Caithness terms they might have been known as the 'orra man'.[7] Compare this with the Caithness farms such as Clyth Mains, which in 1861 had three shepherds, one grieve,[8] four ploughmen, ten agricultural labourers and one domestic servant.

The workers in Patagonia were, on the whole, well provided for. While the workers' revolution of the early 1920s was supposedly about seeking better conditions, the argument seems to have applied in only certain cases.

A typical estancia worker's menu might be:

Breakfast: coffee with milk, bread and butter and steak.

Lunch: soup, stew and coffee.

At 4 o'clock: coffee with milk and bread.

Twice a week, at least, dessert.[9]

By and large many of the Patagonian sheep farmers had risen through the 'worker' status and knew only too well how important it was to ensure good food and accommodation for their men. The Caithness Patagonian Pioneers had learned to survive either on what they could catch, or to eke out what little they had. A true Caithness spirit of course prevailed that always saw the glass half full rather than half empty; a 21st-century descendent remembers her grandfather explaining how he coped: 'as long as I had a bittie o' hard breid in ma pocket'.

Scots were particular about their Patagonian farms, and it was claimed that the Scots were the best farm managers. Across their farms there was 'not a post out of true'. Caithnesian John Hamilton was particularly recognised for his business acumen, and the firm of Hamilton & Saunders offered a model for others to follow.

John Hamilton had been among the first of the Patagonian sheep farmers, and as we have seen he had been an integral part of the 'great trek' that brought thousands of sheep to Patagonia. In 1889 he and Thomas Saunders, another Scottish entrepreneurial emigrant, formed a partnership that established sheep farms in the region of Rio Gallegas in Patagonia.

Today the Hamilton farms of Morro Chico and Pali Aike continue to be run by Hamilton's descendants, a testimony to his business acumen. He had a keen sense of where the best sheep farming land lay, and possessed the entrepreneurial skills to invest in and build extremely successful businesses. The company, Hamilton & Saunders, commenced with 22 leagues purchased at a cost of $1,200 gold pesos per league:

> 1893 their business sheared 42000 sheep and they owned 58 square leagues of land, of which 20 leagues were paid in full and the mortgage on the rest was in such shape as to give them no uneasiness ... the sale of wool from these 42000 sheep earned them $42000 gold clean profit, above all expenses.[10]

In an attempt at diversification, John Hamilton set up a seal oil production programme, which was ultimately not very successful, although there were a number of seal 'factories' in Patagonia. John Hamilton may well have known that seal oil had once been a Caithness export and had long been used in crusie lamps[11] throughout Caithness, to light the homes.

Hamilton also introduced onto his Falkland Islands properties animals such as foxes, skunks, otters and guanacos for their pelts and skins. Uniquely, he brought Shetland ponies and Highland cattle onto his Falklands properties.

The first consignment of ponies came from Scotland, but had to be destroyed on arrival following an outbreak of anthrax on the ship. Later shipments of Shetland ponies were delivered, but Hamilton was unable to personally supervise the purchase of them, and questioned the pedigree of the stock.

Foxes were the plague of Patagonian sheep farmers and given that the original

Falklands foxes had been declared extinct in 1876, their introduction seemed a strange decision by Hamilton, himself a sheep farmer.

The guanaco industry never really flourished (although many of these animals remain on Staats Island in the Falklands). The Highland cattle and Shetland pony experiments only lasted while Hamilton was alive and took an interest in them.

Much of John Hamilton's legal and financial business was conducted from his hometown of Wick, through the firm of Georgeson & Son. Wick was of course a long way away, and communication often necessitated the use of telegrams to conclude and inform urgent business. Local Patagonian business support services were also required, and travelling accountants would visit the estancias. One firm, Lethaby & Gallie, also had a northern Scotland connection. The Gallie family had originated from Tain in Ross-shire, and Andrew Gallie headed up the business based in Rio Gallegas, dealing with nearly everything that the estancias needed; the range of business activities included sheep dip, windmills, water pumps and the Leyland agency. Alexander MacKay Gallie, who had arrived in Punta Arenas in 1920 to join his brother's firm, had married John Hamilton's eldest daughter, Olive. With her early and untimely death, Alexander Mackay Gallie was to play a significant role in the business affairs of Hamilton & Saunders.

At various times due to government restrictions, it was difficult to transfer money out of Argentina. Ways were of course found around this. John Hamilton was able to use his income to set up the John Hamilton Trust, designed to support businesses setting up in Caithness. We know that he also financially assisted the cash flow problems of his brother Daniel, who owned a hardware store the USA. Undoubtedly, John Hamilton had business interests beyond Argentina; he seems to have been an agent for a Belgian bank and he invested in land on the Falkland Islands. So in his case the opportunities to shift money may have been easier than it was for others.

Family money seems also to have been sent home by the Bain family to help support their parents at Mavesy in Lybster. Esperanza House in Halkirk was the property of the Caithness Patagonian pioneer Angus MacPherson, although it might be noted that Angus also spent a successful time owning a cattle ranch in Canada.

The Bain Brothers were to become significant Patagonian sheep farmers. William had been the first of the brothers to arrive in Patagonia, in 1896. Initially he signed up with Mauricio Braun to manage and develop Estancia Josefina, where some 25,000 sheep were to be kept. William later bought the farm, and to the present day Estancia Josefina continues to be farmed by the family.

Donald, Angus Robert and George followed their older brother William to Patagonia, where they formed a partnership with two other Caithness brothers, Robert and Donald Nicolson, to develop Estancia Hercules. It appears that Robert Nicolson was also the custodian of a Nicolson Patagonian investment from his native Clyth. His letters home tell of him trying to find a buyer for Patagonian sheep.

Donald Nicolson was to eventually be the sole lessee of Estancia Hercules, while in 1912 the Bain Brothers leased the 20,000 hectares of Estancia 81.

Partnership and support among the Caithness Pioneers was obviously important, especially when family was involved. William Bain offered sheep to Robert Nicolson. Later, Robert Nicolson encouraged and recruited James MacKay from Geislittle, near Thurso in Caithness, to go to Patagonia. Add to that three Hendry brothers, two Sutherland brothers and William Budge, all in some way neighbours or relatives of the Bains of Mavesy.

This list of land holdings by some of the early Caithness Pioneers is worth tabulating:

- William Bain leased 9,803 hectares in 1915
- John MacLeod leased 6,230 hectares
- John Cormack leased 20,000 hectares in 1909
- Robert MacDonald leased 25,000 hectares in 1907
- John Hamilton owned c. 23,000 hectares in 1888
- Hamilton & Saunders owned c. 70,000 hectares from about 1887
- Hamilton & Saunders leased 6,045 hectares in 1907
- Angus Robert Bain owned 2,500 hectares before 1914
- George Bain owned 2,500 hectares before 1914
- Donald Nicolson owned 2,500 hectares before 1914.[12]

One of the first tasks on setting up an estancia was to erect fencing as a demarcation between neighbouring farms. The Bain Brothers faced a huge task in putting up wire fencing along the six linear leagues that marked them off from four other farms.[13]

Sheep was the prime product of Patagonian farms, and much of the land was, and still is, little suited to the growing of much in the way of crops. Yet some crops were grown. John Cormack on his farm at Mendi Aike kept: 'oxen for plowing to sow oats, which served as fodder for the winter'.[14]

There seems to have been an unwritten law that if a house appeared between sunset and sunrise the plot could be claimed. John Cormack from Achow, Swiney, near Lybster in Caithness, arrived in Patagonia around 1895 and worked initially for John Hamilton. In order to establish his own farm, Cormack built a wooden house on four leagues of land at North Hills, on what was supposedly government reserved land. Soon afterwards he was informed that he had to leave, as the land actually belonged to Hamilton & Saunders. His family have always protested the legality of this move, but at the time he had no choice but to move again and leave behind everything that could not be carted.

John Cormack then set about re-establishing himself and bought 12 leagues of land at Mendi Aike, some 40 miles from Rio Gallegas.[15] While building the new house he slept in a tent on the land, while members of his family were housed in the White

Elephant Hotel in Rio Gallegas. The Cormack family was a victim of land selling again in 1934, and once more they were forced to uproot and start over once more.

From the perspective of those who had worked hard to develop the farms, this was a disaster. The new owners seemed to care little. John Pilkington in his 'Englishman in Patagonia' quotes Margaret Harper, daughter of Wick man John Harper, as saying: 'The peasants let the pigs in the kitchen garden … The pigs ate the vegetables while the people bought vegetables in town.'[16]

In later years, as land became more of a commercial, and indeed a political, commodity the rights to the plots of land were challenged. Acquiring a plot of land in Patagonia in the early days of the pioneers seemed to be based on squatter's rights or the ability to pay the government significant sums of money. Some owners of Patagonian estancias were able to buy land in the early days for as little as 8 cents per acre.

As the Argentine government became more aware of the economic potential of Patagonian land, it became more difficult to acquire land at the previous low prices. Government regulations were enacted that effectively meant that applications were required for the purchase plots of land, and an assessment would be made as to a person's 'suitability'. David Barnetson, for example, applied for a plot, but his application failed; the reason given was that at the time he had a broken leg.

Among the many 'reforms' introduced by President Perón's government during the 1950s was a deliberate breakup of the large farms. They were divided into parcels of 8 leagues, and 'loyal' workers were given 2 leagues each. In this way a number of managers of the larger farms became farmers in their own right. Patagonia had until the era of Perón been largely ignored in terms of government and politics. However with Perón and Evita's declared support for workers and their rights, all areas of Argentina became more politically aware and active.

As ownership, and consequently income, increased, a number of the Caithness Patagonians began to make trips back home. Caithness must have been in their minds regularly. Whether sitting alone in a shepherd's hut or relaxing after a hard and successful day's shearing, the thoughts of our pioneers must have often turned to visualising the land they left behind; mind's-eye pictures of the croft they grew up on, the family and friends they left behind, must have been commonplace. For some, this would have led to a yearning to go home – some permanently, others to visit – and maybe for others, if they had in fact run away from something, grateful thanks that they were now safe and away from whatever challenges their erstwhile home had presented.

Access to ship passenger lists has greatly improved in recent years, and a study of those travelling between Britain and South America reveals that a number of our Caithness Patagonian Pioneers were making fairly regular trips back and forth across the Atlantic. Liverpool and Southampton were the main British ports of both departure and arrival, while on the other side of the Atlantic Buenos Aires was the main Argentinian port and Punta Arenas the predominant Chilean base.

Over time many of the descendants of the original Caithness Pioneers became Argentine citizens, and as a consequence Spanish became their native language – although when the original husband and wife pioneers were both Scottish, integration into the more mainstream Argentine society and culture naturally took a bit longer. To this day there remain distinct traces of Scottish and Caithness words and phrases in their discourse; for example, Bobby Bain continues to have a number of Caithness words and phrases in his vocabulary – not many people in Patagonia can successfully call a dog a 'dowg'. He also talked about the 'coos in e byre'. It is also the turn of phrase that makes the Caithness connection; when Helen Bain (née MacKay) said, 'Lord, lassie, I hope you never want', this conjures up a picture of a wise woman who has experienced life but retained her roots.

A number of Caithness Patagonian descendants continue to talk about Caithness as 'home', yet at best they have only been there on a visit. Like all meetings with long-lost or never-met relations, these trips to Caithness are fondly remembered. Helena Bain has strong memories of making a trip to the original family croft at Mavesy, and Diana MacPherson was only four years old when she visited her family in Thurso, but remembers being fascinated by a cousin drawing on the blackboard in the Station Hotel. The outbreak of the First World War prevented David Barnetson from returning to Caithness. His subsequent marriage to a 'local Argentinian lass', Maria Cozzetti, the birth of his family and basically life meant he never had the opportunity again. David eventually became an Argentine citizen. However, his granddaughter, Margarita, did make a trip to Caithness.

---

1 *Dusk on the Campo*/Sara Mansfield Taber Henry Holt 1992.
2 *Idle Days in Patagonia*/ W. H. Hudson.
3 National Archives of Scotland -GD1/987.
4 Pablo Beecher interview notes.
5 *Patagonia, A Forgotten Land: from Magellan to Perón*/ C.A Brebbia. WIT Press. 2006.
6 *New Zealand Tablet*, 1883.
7 Odd-job man.
8 More or less equivalent to a general foreman/bailiff.
9 *Cómo se trabaja en las estancias patagónicas* – http://patlibros.org/lpa/vwoth/como-se-trabaja.htm
10 *The Gold Diggings of Cape Horn*/ John R Spears. 2012.
11 Small oil lamps with a free-floating wick and a lower pan to catch overflowing oil; fish or animal oils or fats were burnt in them, and they were smoky and smelly, and gave little light – but they were all that the people could afford.
12 Los duenos de la tierra en la Patagonia austral 1880–1920.
13 Los Bain: Del Mar del Norte a la Patagonia.
14 Pablo Beecher interview notes.
15 Club Britannica Rio Gallegas.
16 *An Englishman in Patagonia*/John Pilkington.1991.

Family Life

After arrival on the land, the family home had to be built. In size and extent, houses tended to reflect the status of the owners. The architecture was often a mix of Scottish country house and more traditional Argentine styles. The prevailing local conditions had a significant bearing on the house's layout; protection from the cold and the wind was paramount: 'the settling of the ranch acquires the characteristics of a refuge which must fulfill the basic requirements of self-sufficiency'.[1]

Many families ensured they had a garden. It provided a practical source of fresh fruit and vegetables, of course, but it was also a psychological statement of an oasis in the wilderness. John MacLeod, originally from Clyth in Caithness, effectively brought his house from home. Once established in the Bahia Laura area, he shipped the various sections of the house from Britain before assembling it on his farm. Given the scarcity of local raw materials and the distance involved in land transportation, the option of having the kits delivered by sea from Britain was relatively economic.

This practice of shipping whole buildings had been in operation on the Falkland Islands since 1849, when 30 Chelsea Pensioners and their families had been encouraged to settle on the islands.[2] In 1873 an iron church was shipped from Scotland to the town of Darwin on East Falkland.[3]

Once married, the Caithness Patagonian Pioneers settled down to family life, and for most, children naturally followed. Giving birth in some of the more isolated estancias must have been traumatic and no doubt worrying. Medical help was often a long way away, so women relied on their closest neighbours for support. Whenever possible, expectant mothers would make their way to towns such as Rio Gallegas in advance of their due date.

With few exceptions, the children of the Caithness Patagonian families were born in Patagonia. However, Elizabeth (née Sinclair), wife of William Bain, made the journey all the way back home to her family near Lybster for the birth of a daughter, Jessie MacGregor Bain.

While the child could only have remained for a short time in Caithness, she must have felt some affinity with the place, for the young Jessie Bain accompanied her mother and father on two trips back there. She later, as Jessie Cormack Bain, also gave birth in Caithness; illness struck her while in Patagonia and, accompanied by her husband David Bain, she returned to her family home in Lybster where she gave birth to a son, Donald Allan Cormack Bain – and she never got well enough to return to Patagonia. Another exception was Angus McPherson, who had married while in Canada, and between returning from North America and *en route* back to Patagonia, a son, William Robert McPherson, was born to him in Halkirk.

Alexander Nicol left Wick for Patagonia sometime after 1901. He returned to Wick in 1910 to marry Janet Nicolson, also from Wick. At the time of his marriage he was listed as a ranchman, although he was later employed in an administrative capacity at the refrigeration plant Frigorifico Bories. A son, James Peter Nicol, was born in Rio Gallegas in 1911, but mother and son returned to Wick in 1913. It is not difficult to see why they returned home to Wick in 1913 if the living conditions were anything like those described by Tom Jones:

There was an iron bath in a lean-to and taking a weekly bath meant paying the watchman to bring two buckets of hot water from the boiler house. In the winter months one broke the ice on the water in the jug in the bedroom before beginning one's ablutions.[4]

In Caithness the naming of children was important. A fairly strict rule was applied whereby children were named after grandfathers and grandmothers, sometimes to their longer term embarrassment. If the sequence required the name to commemorate a grandfather, many a female child ended up with the suffix 'ina', so Jamesinas and Robertinas abound, and many of those born in Patagonia continued this tradition. Among the Bain family there is the frequent use of the middle name MacGregor as a remembrance of Jessie MacGregor, the mother of the seven original Bain pioneers. In the same way, the son of Donald Bain and Helen Ross was named David Ross Bain. David Barnetson remembered his brother Ephraim with a son of the same name. John and Williamina McKinnon's daughter, Colina MacDonald McKinnon, was named after Williamina's mother, Colina MacDonald.

The Patagonian homes of the Caithness Pioneers were some distance from sources of provisions. The cost of transporting what we would call staple items, such as meat, eggs, poultry and fish, was consequently very high. There was also some level of exploiting the laws of supply and demand to push up the price of these items. On the plus side, life on an estancia meant that homegrown and farm-produced food was plentiful. A Doctor Fenton, writing to his mother, pointed out that he had the advantage of such fare:

The simple necessaries of life, meat, fish, fowl, eggs, bread, etc., cost little or nothing, I can kill a fat sheep when I wish … which are very good eating … with fresh butter and milk and a good barrel of claret.[5]

Not surprisingly mutton was something of a staple diet among those on the estancias. Other native animals also provided an alternative diet. The armadillo, cooked in its shell, was considered succulent and tender; the flesh resembles pork and is considered a delicacy. The rhea provides a range of options from its eggs, gizzard, wings and body flesh. The following descriptive culinary piece provides all you need to know in the preparation of the rhea:

> To cook it Indian fashion, the bird is plucked and stones heated; it is then laid on its back and drawn; the legs are carefully skinned down and the bones taken out, leaving the skin; the carcass is then separated into two halves, and the back bone having been extracted from the lower half, and the meat sliced so as to admit the heated stones laid between the sections, it is tied up like a bag, secured by the skin of the legs, with a small bone thrust through to keep all taut. This is placed on the live embers of the fire, a light blaze being kindled when it is nearly done to perfectly roast the outside meat. It must be turned frequently. When ready it is taken off the fire, and the top part being cut off and the stones extracted the broth and meat are found deliciously cooked. When the head and breast part are to be cooked the bone is not extracted, but the wings turned inside, and the breast cavity filled with heated stones and tied up with half of the skin of the legs, which have been divided, additional pieces of meat from the legs having been placed in the breast cavity.

Eating is an important part of family life in Patagonia; a full-scale *asado* (traditional barbecue) is a sight not only worth seeing but a delight to taste.

Illness struck Patagonian families, as it does all families, but here isolation and distance from doctors meant that medical support was often difficult to access. Patagonia benefited greatly from the medical services of the Fenton family. Arthur Fenton did his rounds on horseback, as did his brothers, Victor and then George. However the vastness of Patagonia could never have allowed any doctor to adequately cover the whole area, so people often turned to other sources of help. There were instances of families being helped by the native peoples, in terms of natural cures and childbirth, although the native way of applying massage to the whole body was maybe not adopted. There were some midwives, but generally women would rely either on their nearest neighbours or ensure they moved to the nearest town in time for the birth. In the case of more minor situations, help was on hand for cuts and bruises by rubbing them with raw mutton.

The concept of neighbours is somewhat different to the experiences of those of us in our crowded Western civilisation. In Patagonia, the nearest might be many kilometres away, yet on horseback and by cart it was always possible to make visits. In Puerto Deseado, a Ladies' Benevolent Society was established with the aim of providing some level of medical attention.

The Welsh people that settled in the Chubut region of Patagonia deliberately established a community where they would know their neighbours. The Caithness Patagonian Pioneers were, however, much more widely dispersed, working on and owning estancias wherever the opportunity came along. So for them, having Caithness neighbours could be little more than chance. When John Cormack settled his family at Mendi Aike, they found one of the neighbouring families to be the MacDonalds at Estancia La Vanguardia; Robert MacDonald was a native of Strath Halladale in Sutherland.

La Vanguardia was acquired by Robert MacDonald in 1900. His death at sea saw his plans for a model establishment delayed, but his wife, Doña Fernanda (née Garcia), took over these plans and developed La Vanguardia into a very successful estancia, with some 27,000 sheep.

Robert MacDonald had left Scotland for Patagonia at the age of 16, and was originally employed as a shepherd by John Hamilton at the Hamilton & Saunders estancia of Otway Station. He worked for seven years and then as a manager at Estancia Ruben Aike. He married Doña Fernanda Garcia in 1896. It was on a trip back to Britain that he died in July 1920, on board ship. He left seven children.

When illness became more serious, families were left to manage as best they could. In one extreme instance, the wife had to perform the ghastly tasks of undertaker, gravedigger and minister for her dead husband.[6] Distance from towns meant that many graveyards were established on estancia land. In 1921, three of John and Williamina MacKinnon's children died in Patagonia; it proved the final straw for the McKinnon family, so they returned to Caithness.

Education has long mattered to the Scots, and a range of solutions ensured that the children in Patagonia were well taught. Caithness Patagonian families, depending on their location and ability to pay, either educated their children at home or in towns and cities. Some children went to boarding schools in Britain. It must have been fairly momentous for these children, having to live potentially long distances away from their parents. One Scot, Roderick Munro, and his wife, who lived on the Falkland Islands, made the decision to take the whole family back to Scotland in order to ensure their children received an education to their standards.

The relative isolation of many of the estancias meant that for some families schools were out of reach, and instead they employed family-based tutors. Scotland was a key source for these tutors, as this advertisement from *The Scotsman* shows:

TUTOR – wanted for sheep farmer's family in Southern Patagonia: salary, £50 per annum, with board, etc.: free passage out and back: three years engagement: must be able to teach piano. Address, with copies of testimonials and all particulars

Another family was seeking a governess for their children:

GOVERNESS – wanted in September for Patagonia, to teach boy and girl, 9 and 7 years; three years agreement. Apply, Miss Peet, 10 Drumsheugh Gardens, Edinburgh.[7]

Caithness Patagonian couple George and Helen Bain (née Mackay) employed a live-in tutor for their children; her major remit was to teach the children English. While English, or at least English with a Caithness dialect, was used at home, many of those around them would be Spanish speakers, so it was important for these families that the children were given an 'English' education. Meanwhile, stories are told of how the Scottish children's lack of Spanish at local schools meant that both teachers and fellow pupils made fun of them. However, Bobby Bain, son of Caithness Patagonian pioneer Angus Robert Bain, remembers attending school in the town of Trelew, where lessons were conducted in Spanish in the morning and English in the afternoon.

George Bain made the appointment of their live-in tutor during a trip to Scotland in 1929. Miss Christian Judge, a 30 year-old teacher from Avoch on the Black Isle near Inverness, sailed to Patagonia in September 1929 with the Bain family. She remained with the Bain family until 1933, when she returned to her native home and continued as a teacher on the Black Isle.

Caithness Patagonian John Cormack also brought a teacher into his home. Walter MacNay from England had been recommended as 'an intelligent' man. John Cormack met him and was impressed enough to give him employment. The importance of education is exemplified by the fact that John then built a school on his farm (remember there were 11 children in the family) and kitted it out with:

desks with inkwells made of lead; teacher's desk; the board and also a blackboard for each of us, they wrote with a finite black pencil, which we erased with a sponge.[8]

The children attended the school from 9 to 12 in the morning and again from 2 to 4 in the afternoon. Saturdays were not excluded, as they were set aside for drawing and painting. The children even had homework.

When the children grew older, many were sent to boarding schools in Buenos Aires. While some boarded with relatives in the city, it must have been somewhat traumatic for these young people.

The grandchildren of Caithness Patagonian Elizabeth (née Sinclair), wife of William Bain, fondly remember how they used to enjoy visiting this remarkable lady during the times she spent living in Buenos Aires. Meeting her for tea in a restaurant was especially rewarding.

The schools most commonly attended by the Pioneers' offspring and descendants were St George's College for Boys, St Andrew's Scots School for Boys, Quilmes High School for Girls and St Hilda's College. These are well-established private schools serving the educational needs and beliefs of parents. The Saint Andrews Scots School, as the name suggests was, and continues to be, favoured by families of

Scottish descent. Children from a number of the Caithness families became board-ing pupils at these schools

The boarding school attended by some of the Cormack children was a 'Mary Help of Christians School' that was owned and run by the Salesian Sisters, and where rules were strictly enforced. John Cormack, too, believed in the enforcement of rules during schooling; he gave his family tutor *carte blanche* in respect of enforcing school rules, and assured him that he would back up his decisions. This firmness was witnessed by one on the receiving end:

We have to help clean and do other things. Once I was asked to take shopping to the kitchen and I dropped and broke the package lentils. I had to put together one by one 'to again be more careful'.[9]

The schools established under the Salesian order were originally intended for the education of the young people from the native tribes, and to that end a number of schools across Patagonia were founded. In fact the Salesian order was a major force in the civilisation of Patagonia.

In Punta Arenas an English language school was established in 1904. Originally called St James' College it was open to both British and Chilean children. Run very much on British education lines, in the 1930s it ran admission exams for English universities. Following a number of financial challenges the college was renamed The British School of Punta Arenas. Margaret Harper, the daughter of John Harper, a Caithness Patagonian from Wick, was to become one of the school's teachers. She was also recognised for her knowledge of the history of the area.

Sending your children to a Buenos Aires school meant them being away from home, but at least some form of termly or occasional contact was still possible. Some Caithness Patagonian families decided, however, that their children should be educated in Britain; John and Olivia Hamilton enrolled their two daughters, Olive and Penelope, at Lansdowne House School in Edinburgh.

Lansdowne House was a private all-girls school. Established in 1879, it became home for Olive Hamilton until 1927, while her sister Penelope remained there a further two years. Today it continues as one of the few all-girls schools in Scotland, and now operates under the name of St George's School for Girls. John Hamilton and his wife Olive made regular trips to Britain, combining business with visits to the girls. Hamilton's solicitor and agent D. W. Georgeson took an active interest in the welfare of the Hamilton girls, and acted as an information route between the girls and their parents.

William Begg, who had originally left Caithness in 1891, also sent his children back to Britain for their education. He had married Martha Harriet Munday in Patagonia in 1896. Martha was originally from Ewelme in Oxfordshire, and this no doubt influenced their educational choice. If Martha had attended the local Ewelme school she would have been educated in an idyllic English countryside, with a rich heritage to match.

The Munday family name is still recognised in the village, although there is a legend that claims that the Munday family carried the consequences of a curse placed on a mother by a local witch. The effect was to severely cripple her sons![10] In 1901 Martha sailed back to Britain with their four oldest children, some of them never to return to Patagonia.

Even at an early age, children could be sent to school in Britain. Santiago Earsman, son of Caithnesian James Earsman, went to school in Scotland as a small boy, and he remained there until he reached the age of 12. His memories are of sadness at being parted from his family.

Two Caithness Patagonian children received their early education in Caithness. Anita and Jessie Bain, daughters of Donald Bain and Helen Ross were brought up in Lybster by their grandparents. Their mother Helen Ross died during the birth of a daughter, Elena, in 1927. These two older sisters were despatched to their grandparents' home in Lybster. Apparently when they returned to Patagonia for the holiday periods they pined for Lybster! Both eventually settled in Argentina.

A lasting legacy from Caithness to Patagonian education exists in the form of a school in the town of Perito Moreno, built on land donated by Caithness Patagonian pioneer Angus MacPherson. The inhabitants of the town subsequently acknowledged his generosity during a ceremony in 1931, when a housing complex was named in his honour.

Current links have also been established between Lybster Primary School in Caithness and Malvinas Argentinas Primary School in Fitzroy, Santa Cruz province. Lybster was of course, where many of the Caithness Pioneers had attended school. Malvinas Argentinas School has a significant link back to the Bain family. A granddaughter of William Bain attended the school as a child, then on qualifying as a teacher became its sole teacher for some years.

Currently both schools have children that are descended from another Caithness family line. Fitzroy, like Lybster, is a relatively small village and its school provides for the children of the village and the surrounding farms. While the two sets of pupils use different languages it is hoped that each may learn a little of the other's.

Families tended to be fairly large, so even in an isolated place there would always have been siblings to play with. The winter in Patagonia can be harsh, but snow brings the potential for sledging and other snow-based fun; John Cormack's children were assisted by their live-in teacher to make skates and sledges out of whatever was around the home. As they grew into teenagers and young men and women, however, life on the farm could be a bit stifling. Nevertheless all of the family would be involved in sheep farming and all would be competent horse-riders.

Of course there were families and friends who were left behind in Caithness. Some of the Caithness Patagonian Pioneers never saw their Caithness family and friends again. As transport improved and families became more established, trips to the homeland increased, for some. As we have seen, many returned to Caithness to marry, so some sweethearts would only have been parted for short periods, but the extent to which these future husbands and wives knew each other remains uncertain. In a number of cases, the prospective husbands arrived in Caithness, were married and within a short time were off again. This suggests some form of longer-term association.

Parents however must have felt the loss. Knowing that your son or daughter was setting off into the unknown must have been difficult, and the thought that you might never see them again must also have weighed heavily. For example, David Barnetson never returned home. and this must have been a sore loss for his parents.

Many did return. Some permanently, and others on visits back home. One of the regular travellers was Robert Nicolson, who returned regularly to Lybster during the Caithness summer months. In Patagonia, of course, it was winter at that time, and whenever possible Patagonians either 'hibernate' or depart during these cold winter months. Robert Nicolson would set up residence in the Portland Arms Hotel, Lybster, where a car was kept for him. In this he would 'perambulate' around the county.

Percy Earsman was also a fairly regular traveller across the Atlantic, spending time both in Caithness and with his wife's Sutherland family. In 1923 all three of the Earsman brothers were back in Scotland, maybe for a family event. George Bain and his wife Helen MacKay, both from Caithness, made a couple of trips. Sinclair Sutherland from Lybster, at one point, decided to move back to Caithness but when he arrived he found he no longer knew anyone so returned to Patagonia. Similar thoughts must have gone through Elizabeth Bain's mind when her family suggested a trip to coincide with her 70th birthday. She declined, as she felt there was nobody there that she would know. Today a number of third- and fourth-generation families make something of the occasional 'pilgrimage' to the land of their fathers and mothers.

The original Caithness Patagonians usually signed a five-year contract, and no doubt many expected to come home again following completion of their contract. Some did indeed return, generally because they were unsettled in the new land. Circumstances outwith their control also played a part; war in Europe was to impact on three of the Caithness Pioneers.

David Barnetson had planned a trip to Caithness, but due to the outbreak of the First World War such a voyage was difficult and considered unsafe. The Hendry brothers, George and William, returned to Scotland in 1915. William eventually returned to Patagonia, but George was killed in action in France in 1918. William Budge made the decision in 1941 to return to Britain to join the Second World War forces, and served in a tank regiment in Africa.

For those family and friends still in Caithness, there must have been a keenness to keep in touch. Letters were written, but by the time they reached their destination news may well have been 'old news'. Prior to the introduction of regular mail services it might be as few as four times a year that any mail was delivered or uplifted. Angus MacPherson, in his diaries, bemoans the lack of mail; there is an entry that records his depression caused by loneliness, and he questions whether or not he even deserves any mail.

The *Amadeo*, a steamer built in Britain, operated in the Magellan Strait between 1890 and 1932, and was something of a lifeline for the shepherds, miles from any town or in regular contact with home. The *Amadeo* was in effect the mail boat, and if you were lucky it brought a letter from home. Today it lies as a wreck, poignantly opposite the now equally dilapidated Estancia San Gregoria, once one of the largest of Patagonia's sheep farming establishments.

The time it took to transport the mail back to Scotland, along with the uncertainty of when the Patagonian mail boat would arrive to collect the letters, made important communications difficult. Jessie Bain, the mother of the Bain brothers and sisters in Patagonia, died suddenly at the family home in Mavesy in 1920, at a time when most of her children were far away. Trips home following such tragic events must have been difficult to arrange at short notice, and emotionally upheaving when travel was not possible.

Some local newspapers, such as the *Magellan Times*, were published in English as populations grew in the Patagonian towns. For those in the more remote estancias, a popular and keenly looked-for mail packet might contain newspapers from home. We know that George Bain's family received the *Groat* from time to time, and from a quote in Angus MacPherson's diary we can surmise that he must have had access to the *Press & Journal*, the daily newspaper covering north and east Scotland.

1 *Arquitectura y urbanismo en Iberoamérica*/ Ramón Gutiérrez.
2 The Falkland Islands, 1833–1876: The Establishment of a Colony/ Stephen A. Royle in *The Geographical Journal* Vol. 151, No. 2 (Jul., 1985), pp. 204–214.
3 *Argentina's Rise: the Falkland Islands.* - https://falklandstimeline.wordpress.com/1850-1899/
4 *Patagonian Panorama*/ Tom P. Jones. 1961.
5 http://www.patbrit.org/eng/events/rr1885fenton.htm.
6 *Padre in Patagonia* http://www.electricscotland.com/history/argentina/lecture2.htm.
7 *The Scotsman* 19 July 1930
8 Pablo Beecher interview notes.
9 Pablo Beecher interview notes.
10 *Ewelme: a romantic village*/ E. M. Prister Cruttwell.

The Wild Side

Growth and success brings with it greed and mistrust. In the early 1920s Patagonia was the venue of a workers' revolution. The precursor to more widespread worker dissatisfaction began at the plant known as Frigorifico Bories, near Puerto Natalles, in 1919. This event was to become known as the 'war of the stone throwers', as these were the weapons the workers used to attack the managers of the plant. The dispute erupted over grievances about pay and harsh conditions. The plant was in the joint ownership of a Scotsman named Cameron, who along with his team of managers and administrators, were set upon by the enraged workforce. Caught up in the attack was Alexander Nicol, originally from Wick.

Nicol came to Patagonia sometime around 1900, and by 1919 he was employed as an administrator at Frigorifico Bories. He had been employed as a posting master in Wick prior to leaving for Patagonia, so would have acquired organisational and administrative skills by having to ensure the mail coaches and horses were ready and available as required. During his earlier years in Patagonia he must have gained considerable knowledge of animals, as he was employed at the refrigeration plant as an administrator responsible for the sorting and grading of the incoming live animals. He managed to escape from the plant at the outbreak of the violence, and along with two others was forced to hide among the hills near Estancia Dorotea for some days. The conflict only lasted a short time, but a lengthy legal process occupied many years thereafter. Alexander Nicol's subsequent life remains something of a mystery.

Wide-ranging disgruntlement with wages and conditions at the refrigeration plants began to spread to some estancias, and led to a more widespread workers' revolution in the early 1920s. Conditions that consisted of living in sheds shared with tools and machines, sleeping on hides of sheep, and poor sanitation, along with poor wages, were the stated causes. While many poor workers joined the rebels, a number of their 'leaders' were playing a wider political card. As early as 1917, John Hamilton had been warned that his labourers were thinking about going on strike.

Patagonia may be a far away and often isolated place, but it was still part of the wider world, and news of revolutions in Russia and Mexico at this time may have helped fuel some of the activity.

The first major Patagonian workers' strike seemed to have successfully achieved its aims; the landowners made representations to the government in Buenos Aires and as a result an army under the command of Lieutenant Colonel Varela was sent to Patagonia. Much to the annoyance of many farmers, Varela effectively negotiated a settlement with the strikers that was supposed to ensure they were given a minimum wage, clean accommodation with heat and light, and regular meals. Not too surprisingly – and especially since this was a relatively poor time for many sheep farmers – the landowners and farmers reneged on the agreement, and the whole process of protest and disruption began again.

This time, significant mayhem, robbing and looting ensued. The strikers also began taking prisoner those who they perceived to be against them. Considerable physical damage was done to many of the estancias, with some being set on fire. Fences were destroyed and the sheep stocks became mixed. Scabby sheep mingled with the scab-free flocks, and it took many years before scab was significantly eradicated. To try to protect their commercial interests, many estancia owners united in The Livestock, Commercial and Industrial Association.

The situation was also further confused due to strikers being led by different factions. Antonio Soto, a Spanish anarchist who encouraged the peons to rebel against their bosses, led the socialist pretentions of the revolution. Alongside him was Facón Grande, a worker and a good organiser. Under their command, groups of strikers toured the estancias across southern Patagonia in an attempt to encourage workers to join the strike. At the same time a more hot-blooded individual named El Toscana was leading a more violent-minded group, under the banner of the Red Council. This group simply took what they needed – horses, weapons and so on – from estancias.

Lieutenant Colonel Varela returned with his army, and this time leniency and negotiation were not on his agenda. Despite the fact that El Toscana had been arrested and his group's activities curtailed, Varela and his officers brutally hunted down and killed many of the striking workers. No mercy was shown. Farmers were asked to nominate those who might be saved, while the others, including Facón Grande, were made to dig their own graves before being shot by Varela's firing squads. Antonio Soto escaped. The whole episode has left a bad taste in the memory of many in Argentina. As for the workers, they had their wages cut by one third.

Caithness Patagonian Pioneer John Cormack and his family found themselves in the front line:

One day the strikers passed through Mendi Aike and they took some of the staff by force, except for one who managed to hide. Mummy would tell that they entered the storeroom and they ate the eggs raw. She had no choice but to let them take what they wanted and she asked them not to touch her children. They took the horses and only left the one for the guard. Mummy was expecting Polly and everyone advised that the families shouldn't stay at the estancias, so the Taylors at Barranca Blanca brought us to Gallegas and we stayed at the hotel Londres. Dad stayed at the estancia with that labourer and the schoolmaster.[1]

The diplomat MacLeay informed the Foreign Ministry that the residence of John Cormack British subject was assaulted by strikers armed and mounted the horses and commandeered tanks and shearing machines destroyed. And urges the Argentine government to take protective measures.[2]

It was almost impossible for the farmers not to get embroiled in one way or another. According to descendants of the Bain family, the rebels held David and Angus Robert captive. Angus Robert somehow managed to escape, while David was rescued by the army. The same source tells that William Bain was shot at, but the bullet penetrated no further than his thick overcoat.

Claims and counterclaims have been exchanged as to the extent the estancia owners were involved. Some undoubtedly feared for their lands and their families, and so were most likely to support attempts to put down the insurrection.

When it came to deciding which of the rebels should be spared or not, some estancia owners applied a principle that identified workers being classed as either 'good' or 'irretrievable'. Those that were 'irretrievable' were shot. It is claimed that the Argentine army of the time shot and killed some 1,500 'revolutionaries.' Two soldiers, four policemen, one gendarme and a number of ranch owners and their families also died during the conflict.

Whether Patagonia was any more violent than other areas must remain doubtful. Murders and bank robberies are committed on a worldwide basis, yet two Scots were murdered as part of a bank raid in Puerto Santa Cruz. About 11 p.m. on Sunday, 21 April 1935, two masked robbers murdered a bank accountant, Donald Sutherland, and his assistant, Thomas Veitch Henderson. They found the keys to the safe and proceeded to the house of the manager, Alberto MacQuibban. He lived next door to the bank, but refused to open the safe door. The robbers eventually managed to access the safe and made off with $225,000, leaving MacQuibban and his wife unconscious.[3] Donald Sutherland was from Leith and Thomas Henderson, a native of Jedburgh.

Patagonia is of course famous for its association with Butch Cassidy and the Sundance Kid. Having hightailed it from the United States, when the heat from Pinkerton's Detective Agency began to burn, Butch, Sundance and their lady friend, Etta Place, bought a farm in Chubut Provence. On the 14 February 1905 they allegedly returned to their robbing profession by holding up a bank in Rio Gallegas and making off with some 20,000 pesos. Subsequent research has questioned their involvement in this robbery, yet the meticulous planning of the hold-up fits with their modus operandi.

There is no evidence to suggest that any of the Caithness men or women witnessed the robbery, but given that some of them were regular visitors to Rio Gallegas, it must at least have been a major topic of discussion in the town's British Club.

Speculation as to the end of Butch and Sundance continues and John Pilkington in his book 'An Englishman in Patagonia' offers a theory that they were still around in 1908 and potentially the culprits in a robbery at the Casa Lahusen general store in Comodora Rivadavia?

Caithness Patagonian pioneer William Mackenzie did meet with an untimely and still largely unexplained death in Patagonia during 1947. Legend has it that he was murdered, but a headstone in Rio Gallegas Cemetery suggests that he died in the 'line of duty'. What this 'line of duty' was has not been established, but his burial was organised by the Sociedad Anon Imp. y Exp. de la Patagonia, one of the companies in the Braun Menendez empire. If the Sociedad was his employer, then he presumably died carrying out some employment duty; a memory recalled by his relatives in Caithness points towards his intervention in some dispute which resulted in his death.

Life in Patagonia was certainly volatile. Guns and substantial knives were part of the gaucho's toolkit, and no doubt when tempers flared, either could be used first and questions asked later. The Frenchman Alcide d'Orbigny, who made many observations on the early history of Patagonia, wrote that: 'he once saw a gaucho stop playing cards and sink his knife into an Indian who was annoying him'.[4]

Angus MacPherson at one time had a 'dispute' with a gun – the result being a bullet removed from his leg with hot tweezers.

Argentina has a long and complicated history of waging war. Relations with its neighbour, Chile, were often fractious, and in 1877 the two countries were on the brink of going to war with each other over the ownership of Patagonia. But mostly Argentina was at war with itself.

Argentina never became openly involved in either world war, although on each occasion the inclination was to side with Germany and Italy. During the First World War many British and German people returned to their homelands to join their respective forces.

The Argentine president at that time, Hipolyto Irigoyen, had a particular mistrust of the British and indeed the French, so he was quite happy to sell war materials to Italy. His dislike of the United States was even greater, so when they called for neutral countries to break relations with Germany, Argentina simply ignored the plea and remained ostensibly neutral.

Yet for many expats it was a matter of conscience. William Dickie, a Patagonian pioneer from Aberdeenshire, took it upon himself to encourage young British men to sign up, and his greatest success in terms of recruitment was his own two sons. Many willingly donated to funds designed to support the war relief. The ladies of Rio Gallegas were busy knitting during the Second World War; 359 pullovers for the forces, 68 pairs of pyjamas and 160 pairs of socks were among the items despatched to Britain.[5] Another contribution was the creation of a recipe book whose earnings went into the Red Cross Fund. Copies of this book remain in the hands of descendants of Caithness Patagonian Pioneers. A most interesting donation came from the Swear Box at Rio Seco.

Caithness Patagonian connections with the First World War are few, except for one significant example; George Hendry from Mavesy was killed in action. He served as a sergeant in the 13th Battalion (Scottish Horse) Black Watch, and was killed in France on 4 November 1918. The youngest of the Bain Brothers, David, had joined the Seaforth Highlanders prior to the First World War, and did not arrive in Patagonia until after the war. It was the intention of David Barnetson to return to Caithness in 1914; his brother Ephraim, in Caithness, had been trying to encourage him to return home, but with the outbreak of the First World War travel became difficult and he never made it back to his homeland. Robert Harper returned home to Caithness in 1914, but there is no record of any wartime service. He may well have been exempt, as he worked on the land. The same applies to John Cormack Mowat from Olrig; he returned to Caithness for the final time in 1912 but the war service records for him have not been found.

Military service in Argentina was mandatory. A lottery system operated that assigned a number between 1 and 1,000 to a selection of males between the ages of 18 and 21. Those chosen were then conscripted. As a result of this system, David Barnetson's son Epfrain became a soldier in 1934.

During the Second World War, Argentina again remained officially neutral, although its sympathies lay with the Axis countries. President Perón was known to have studied and modelled his governing methods on that of Mussolini. Argentina eventually broke off relations with Germany in 1944. Rumours abounded that many of the Nazi command found sanctuary in Argentina after the war, and to this day there is a hillside in Patagonia where it is claimed that Hitler sat, looking longingly across the Atlantic Ocean.

The only known Caithness Patagonian connection with the Second World War lies with William Budge. He returned from Patagonia in 1941 to Britain and served as a sergeant in Africa.

1 Club Britannica Rio Gallegas.
2 La Patagonia Rebelde./ Osvaldo Bayer, 2004
3 http://patbrit.org/eng/events/scrobbery.htm.
4 *Patagonia, A Forgotten Land: from Magellan to Perón*/ C. A. Brebbia. WIT Press. 2006.
5 Argentine British Community Council.

Social and Community Life

Social life was at best sporadic and often limited for those living on the more distant estancias. Trips to the town coincided with sheep farming business such as the delivery of the bales of wool to the ports or the livestock shows and sales organised by the rural societies. Such opportunities to meet, relax and maybe reminisce about their Caithness homelands were important occasions. Key venues for these gatherings were the British Clubs established in most of the Patagonian towns. It is said that any new person that arrived from Caithness had to firstly have their ancestry dissected and fully understood.

In the towns such as Punta Arenas and Rio Gallegas, clubs were instituted. The British Club in Punta Arenas began in 1899 with membership open only to British males. In the style of a gentleman's club, it offered a bar, a library and billiard tables. The club closed in 1981 due to lack of membership.

The British Club in Rio Gallegas was established in 1911 and served as an important meeting place for sheep farmers. Among the names on the list of members we find these Caithness Patagonian Pioneers:

Angus Bain: David Bain: Donald Bain: George Bain: William Bain: David Barnetson: John Cormack: James Earsman: John Hamilton: W. Hendry: Robert MacDonald: James MacKay: Angus MacPherson: Hugh MacPherson: Robert Nicolson: Donald Nicolson: John Oman: George Plowman.

The club also became a centre for family and children's activities. As the children grew up in the relative isolation of the far-Patagonian Pioneers estancias, when they were 'released' there was a clear need to provide focused activities for them. Otherwise, as Mary Jane Rudd claimed in her diary, high jinks were likely. Mary Jane and her sister allegedly: 'made a hen drunk'.[1]

The club also provided a more sombre function when used as a funeral parlour.

The British Club in San Julián is fondly remembered in relation to Caithness Patagonian pioneer Alexander MacKenzie. Alexander, due to a throat disorder, had lost his voice and took to pen and paper as his means of communication. Apparently he particularly revelled in writing somewhat risqué stories and jokes, which he shared with other visitors to the San Julián British Club.

While the British Clubs served as a meeting place, other organisations were also formed to aid or encourage greater integration into Patagonian society. One aspect of the prevailing culture in Patagonia was the differing languages. Increasingly there were moves for Patagonia to be 'Argentinian', and to that end branches of the Patriotic League were established and supported primarily by businessmen and estancia owners.

The Patriotic League in Santa Cruz province was to be closely involved in and opposed to the workers' strikes of the early 1920s, and estancia owners found themselves being accused of co-operating with the army's policy of firing squads. Following the end of the strikes, the Rio Gallegas Patriotic League canvassed the Argentine government to allow them to hoist the Argentinian flag on Sundays and festive days. The signatories of this motion included two Caithness connections. Representing the estancias of Morro Chico, Punta Loyola and Pali Aike was John Hamilton, and from Estancia La Vanguardia was the family of Robert MacDonald; Robert had died while travelling between Argentina and Britain, but his wife continued to run the farm.

Institutions that were known globally also found some favour in Patagonia. Freemasonry lodges were mainly confined to the more urban areas, and membership tended to be from the professional classes. The Rio Gallegas Lodge was finally dismantled in 1944, but in Punta Arenas the Strait of Magellan Lodge 68, which was formed in 1937, continues to exist. Caithnesian Alexander Nicol is listed as being a member of this lodge in its inception year, 1937.

The Puerto Deseado Rotary Club was, not surprisingly, a mainly British institution that ran a series of benevolent activities.

Agricultural societies and sheep shows were an integral part of the Patagonian farmers' seasonal cycle. Holidays were rare, and these events were looked upon as a chance to get away from the farm, meet with others, and have a good time. Most of the towns established a Rural Society to enable such activities and events. The origin of the Sociedad Rural in Puerto Deseado has strong links with the Bain brothers from Caithness. The first entry in the minute book of the society shows the names of William, George, Angus and Donald Bain among the original 1913 membership. This vital archival resource is also a register of all members from that date. Among the pages, along with references to the Bain brothers, we find entries for Caithnesian brothers Robert and Donald Nicolson, plus Angus MacPherson.

The Sociedad Rural Deseado, like the others, had its own showground and sheep pens. Alongside the serious sheep farming business, this was also a place to meet and exchange stories and experiences. The connection with the Bain family has been preserved and it was chosen as the venue to celebrate 100 years since William, the first of the Bains, had arrived in Patagonia.

In Rio Gallegas the name of John Hamilton heads the list of originators. In 1918 'Don Juan Hamilton' chaired the first Board of the Rural Society of Rio Gallegas and was asked to oversee the re-organisation of the society. The official aims of these societies were, as mentioned earlier, primarily to support the farming businesses. Among the Rio Gallegas Rural Society's aims were:

- The development of livestock rearing
- Improving methods of crop cultivation
- Holding rural exhibitions
- Promoting technical studies and scientific research.

The societies also played a key social role, with dances and various activities organised to coincide with the agricultural shows.

The sound of the bagpipes is dear to the Scot. They announce an arrival, they introduce activity and no doubt they were the sole companions for some as they laboured alone in the vast reaches of Patagonia.

Of our Caithness Pioneers, we know that George and Alexander Plowman were accomplished pipers, much sought after at social gatherings. Dances would be arranged, but males greatly outnumbered the ladies; it was reckoned that in some cases there would be three or four women to a dozen men. Somewhat harshly, it was claimed that some men became defeatist in the hope of finding a lady and became 'not very demanding in terms of beauty and still less in personal aspects'.

This would certainly give credence to why so many men returned to Caithness for wives. The situation in the Falkland Islands had been somewhat more drastic at one time in its early colonisation; the naval officer in charge asked that the islands be supplied with 'six marriageable young women of reputation and character'.[2]

In Rio Gallegas, the Argentino Hotel was considered the most suitable in terms of size for holding significant functions and dances. It was greatly favoured by the sheep farmers and other men of business for conducting and finalising various commercial agreements. Another popular hotel was the White Elephant, which was a favourite stopover on shopping trips. If the 1907 menu is anything to go by, it was well worth a food stop:

Hors d'oeuvres	- Brawn and Tongue
Soup	- Ox Tail
Fish	- Salmon Balls
Entrée	- Stewed Kidney and Mushrooms
Roasts	- Roast Port and Apple Sauce with potatoes
	- Chicken and Scarlet Runners and Brussels Sprouts
Sweets	- Tipsy Cake and Jelly
Cheese	- Gruyere & Dutch

Dessert   *- Almonds and Raisins, Pomegranates, etc.*
Liqueurs   *- Benedictine, Chartreuse and Carabanchel*
Coffee

The White Elephant Hotel was operated between 1900 and 1911 by Edwin Beecher, something of a trailblazer in Patagonia. He was credited with the first car in the region – a British-made Star. By 1929, Patagonian residents proudly owned over 600 cars.

An annual carnival ran in Rio Gallegas, and from the descriptions of the dressing up and the prizes for best costumes. it feels like we have only to think of Gala Week in the Caithness towns and villages to get the idea:

Four friends and another dressed as The Dionne quintuplets who were born in May last year in USA. They managed to get five baby strollers, old gowns, bonnets, baby bottles and pacifiers.[3]

Today, the Caledonian Ball held in July, is a key diary date for those with Scottish connections. Dressing up for these balls was important, especially for the ladies. Daughters of Caithnesian John Cormack, recall the excitement and the importance of getting dresses made that were in the latest European styles.[4]

A necessary social gathering accompaniment, for many Scots, is whisky. Supplies from the homeland would take some time to arrive but the resourceful Scots led by Glasgow based wine and spirits distributing company, Thom and Cameron, imported a brew that they branded 'Tappit Hen'. They set up their Patagonian premises in Puerto Santa Cruz and were the original owners of Estancia Moy Aike Chico, which later belonged to the Halliday family.

Caithness men and women were no doubt well aware of whisky. Rural Caithness had long supported a number of illicit stills. In the early 1820s there were some 200 convictions for unlicensed whisky stills in the County. With the introduction of legislation, authorised distilleries were established at Thurso, Halkirk and Wick. The Wulf Burn Distillery in Thurso was relatively short lived, but has recently been resurrected. Halkirk hosted first the Gerston Distillery and then Ben Morven. Today the main survivor is the Pulteneytown Distillery. It has had a chequered and intermittent history, but now famously produces the Old Pulteney brand.

Whisky was also the alleged downfall of the Sinclairs at the Battle of Altimarlach. Over indulgence on the evening before the battle gave the Campbells of Glenorchy a clear advantage in the ensuing battle.

The Temperance movement found strong support in Caithness during the early part of the 20th century and Wick voted and declared itself 'dry' on 28 May 1922. Approximately 60% of the voting population agreeing with the proposal and the prohibition remained in force for twenty-five years. In Patagonia, the Welsh communities were significant in their aims to remove alcohol from their lives.

It seems reasonable to assume that at least some of the Caithness Pioneers brought this thinking with them. On the other hand there is evidence to suggest that a bottle of Scotch may have been a helpful tonic at times of hardship. Shepherds on their own were the likely candidates for seeking some solace from the bottle. These shepherds often lived in isolated districts, and the Rev. MacColl, one of the Church of Scotland's itinerating ministers, noted that:

> *There is very little companionship of an elevating nature and nearly all the innocent joys and pleasures of life are lacking. Money alone is plentiful, and drink is comparatively cheap; we can understand easily how readily shipwreck can be made of human lives. Yet the cause for wonderment is that so few rather than so many have been overtaken by disgrace.*[5]

Today wine is largely the alcoholic drink of choice, although no Scottish descendant's home is without a bottle of whisky. The Argentinian, however, is unlikely to be far from his *mate*. Central to all working practices, was and is, mate. This caffeine-enriched infused drink is the product of steeped yerba leaves. Mate is a social drink, in that it is shared with each person taking a turn to drink through a silver straw. The gaucho saying tells it all:

> *My mate is my soul-mate. A companion when I am lonely, a comforter when I am troubled and a devoted nurse when I am sick.*[6]

Christmastime was of course a time for the family, and the children eagerly anticipated the arrival of Santa Claus. Christmastime in Patagonia, however, falls during the summer months so for some families it was an ideal time for a picnic. New Year celebrations were important to Scottish settlers, and Auld Lang Syne would ring out across the camp. The granddaughter of Caithness Patagonian pioneer John Cormack describes how it was an integral part of the family's celebration:

> *We went into the garden a few seconds before midnight and Dad pulled the shotgun, shot to the sky to say goodbye to the old year and another to receive the new. It was customary that 'granny' Annie was the first to enter the house and then dad.*[7]

Even if the opportunity to head 'into town' proved not possible, music would ring out from the estancias. If musicians were not available then there was always the gramophone to provide dance music. The petronella and the schottische were noted among the favourite dances. Sundays were a popular day for rolling out the Scottish dance band music. The sword dance was apparently performed in the San Julián British Club. Nevertheless it became fashionable for musicians and orchestras to come from Buenos Aires to play at concerts in the coastal towns.

St Andrew's Day was an important celebration day for the Scottish pioneers. It seems that, unlike at home where Burns Day is the norm, this was an opportunity for the haggis to be prepared. If you had a haggis you also needed a piper, and a Plowman piper from Caithness would be in great demand.

To this day the Highland Games is a feature of the Caithness Patagonian descendant community. Throwing the hammer was an event popular among the Caithness Patagonian Pioneers, with the Plowman brothers being particularly adept. Alexander Plowman, born at the family farm of Balbeg in Spittal, had been a recognised sports figure in the Halkirk area prior to leaving for Patagonia, twice winning the Sir Archibald Sinclair Cup for athletics and also winning the Halkirk Athletic Gold Medal. Many of the Caithness Pioneers would have enjoyed either watching or participating in this popular event. The *John O'Groat Journal*, reporting on the Ackergill Tower Highland Games held in 1880, estimated an attendance of over 3,000– maybe some of the Caithness Patagonian Pioneers attended?

Pride of place in the piping world of Patagonia, however, went to the Plowman brothers. Pictures and stories that survive of Patagonian social events invariably include a Plowman piper. Alex Plowman is remembered as the piper at an Earsman family dance. The younger members of this family were fascinated by this man in a kilt, but thought the bagpipes sounded like 'screeching cats'.[8]

Piping and highland dancing continues to be taught at St Andrew's School in Buenos Aires, and certainly there is a continuing tradition of piping within these Caithness descendant families. Piping instruction in Patagonia, we are told, has even been conducted via the telephone! The current family of MacDonalds who are descended by marriage from Rebecca Bain, originally from Mavesy, are especially accomplished pipers. Their musical heritage comes from their father's family, who belonged to the Hebridean island of Tiree.

The accordion was also a popular instrument among the Caithness Pioneer community, and of course it also has a prominent place in the Argentine tango tradition. The idea of Caithness and Argentinian accordion players creating a fusion of both musical cultures is appealing. Somehow you can just imagine an emotive slow air being used for a tango! It appears however that in reality there was not a great mix of musical cultures.

Radios were also a means of sharing music. Fiddle and bagpipe music were naturally popular amongst the Caithness families, but it was not until 1920 that Argentinian radio was transmitted widely across the country and even then it was necessary to erect a large antenna. An important means of keeping in touch with the outside world was the radio programme *Mensajes para el campo* (*Messages for the Country*).

The people of Argentina are passionate about sport. Horse racing was a common activity on the estancias, where horsemen could display their skills. Polo and show jumping are also Argentinian favourites, and Caithness Patagonian Angus McPherson excelled as a horseman. The family archive holds a picture of Angus on his horse Zino clearing a six-foot jump. He would arrange family polo sessions on his farm at Perito Merino.

The Rio Gallegas racecourse was established in the 1920s. At Puerto Santa Cruz the event would go on for some days with some original-sounding horse-based activities: 'lighting the cigarette, threading the needle, potato race and get down put on a disguise and then remount'.[9]

Gymkhanas were also a favourite opportunity to meet and party. The Rural Society of Rio Gallegos seems to have had a talent for creating quite an event:

In the field there were games with horses and races, lifting potatoes from the soil, circumvent a tour of poles and musical chairs, like the traditional 'musical chairs', except that participants were riding on horses and when the music stopped they had to dismount and sit, those left without a chair, lost. The bar was mounted near the garage.[10]

The Rio Gallegas gymkhanas were originally organised to raise money to support the British Second World War effort, and continued with this philanthropy beyond the end of the war, raising funds for the British Hospital and other institutions.

Soccer is of course a national obsession in Argentina, and Epfrain and Eduardo Barnetson, two sons of Caithness Patagonian Pioneer David Barnetson, became closely involved with the development of Deseado Juniors Football Club. The Barnetson family made significant contributions to the town of Puerto Deseado. Apart from his involvement with the football club, Epfrain also ran the town's newspaper, *El Orden*. David Barnetson owned a hotel in the town and a daughter, Teresa, continued the family tradition of involvement with the Deseado Juniors. In 1936 she used her creative skills to embroider handkerchiefs displaying the colours and logo of the football team.

There also existed a football club in Punta Arenas called the British Athletic Club. In 1898 a football match between Scotland and England took place:

The Scotch team was heavier than the English, but not so fast. After a hard struggle the game resulted in a victory for Scotland—2 goals to 1.[11]

Rugby is also enthusiastically played and followed, and maybe some of the rugby genes came to Patagonia with the Earsmans. John Earsman, father, of the three Caithness Earsmans who went to Argentina, played for Thurso in 1880.

1 *Daily Life on a Patagonian Sheep Ranch*. The private diary of Mary Jane Rudd. 1902.
2 The Falkland Islands, 1833–1876: The Establishment of a Colony/ Stephen A. Royle in *The Geographical Journal* Vol. 151, No. 2 (Jul., 1985), pp. 204–214.
3 http://www.patbrit.org/esp/events/rrhelengooderham.htm.
4 Pablo Beecher interview notes.
5 *Life and Work*: the magazine of the Church of Scotland. 1911.
6 *An Englishman in Patagonia*/ John Pilkington. 1991.
7 Pablo Beecher interview notes.
8 Pablo Beecher interview notes.
9 *The British in Santa Cruz territory 1911–2011*/ María de los Milagros Pierini and Pablo Gustavo Beecher. Edición del Club Británico de Río Gallegos.
10 British Argentine Community Council.
11 *Evening Telegraph* (Dundee), 12 November 1898.

Religious Life

While Caithness was never one of the greatest evangelical regions of Scotland, most faiths and religious denominations have established a base in the county. The First Statistical Account for Caithness quoted the minister in Wick describing the religious disposition of the people as: 'mostly run-of-the-mill members of the established church of Scotland'.

The population have always been church attenders, and religious events, such as the Temperance Movement and the Evangelism among the fishing communities, found voices in the towns and villages of Caithness. John Hamilton's family, for example, are known to have been members of the United Presbyterian Church in Wick. Andrew Key Hamilton, a younger brother of John Hamilton, was named in honour of the then UP Minister, Andrew Key. Having grown up in this environment, the Caithness Patagonian Pioneers and their families would have seen religious observance and belief as important, although it was not a motivating factor in their emigration. In contrast, the Welsh Patagonian settlers chose Patagonia with the intention of making it a place where they could retain their religious customs as a community.

The Patagonian shepherds from Lewis, with their particularly strong religious heritage, were initially recruited by a call from the pulpit. A lovely, but unlikely, legend exists in Patagonia as to how some Scottish shepherds were recruited. Knowing the Scotsman's love of porridge, a bowl of the stuff would be set outside the shepherd's hut and when he popped out to claim it, someone was waiting with a cudgel to knock him out, ready to ship him to Patagonia.[1]

Nevertheless, the men and women from Caithness would have arrived in Patagonia with a bible among their possessions, and undoubtedly with experience of attending their local church. For example, John Earsman, father of William, James and Percy Earsman, was an Elder in Bower Parish Church. His sons were most likely regular attenders during their Caithness youth.

Due to relative remoteness of many estancias, regular church services were unlikely. As we shall see, there is ample evidence of travelling ministers in Patagonia, but it would be relatively normal for a family to engage of some form of religious observance within the family.

Where churches did exist, for example in Punta Arenas, they were almost exclusively Anglican or Roman Catholic, and the Church did send missionaries across the Patagonian region. The government of the Catholic Church in Patagonia was divided into two parts, northern and southern. In the beginning the pioneer work was done by a small band of missionaries trained and guided by the founder of the congregation, John Bosco, an Italian priest, who became known in Patagonia as Don Bosco. He is especially remembered for his work in assisting the establishment of the Patagonian Salesian missions and schools.

The dominance of the Roman Catholic Church created a problem for some of the incoming Scottish families. Mainly of a protestant persuasion, upon death they were excluded from the then public Roman Catholic cemeteries. The consequence was that many of the more remote estancias established their own burial grounds where the workers and their families lie buried. The cemetery at Estancia Josephina is the resting place for a number of the Bain family. Today, in the larger town cemeteries, we find a distinct demarcation between the areas set aside for the two faiths.

The initial Scottish Presbyterian ministry in Argentina dates from 1825, when a group of Scots settlers arrived on the *Symmetry*. When this colony failed to materialise, many of the settlers made their way to Buenos Aires where in 1829 the Scots Presbyterian Church was established, headed by the Rev. William Brown. The Rev. Brown continued his work in Argentina until 1849 when he returned to Scotland, where he took up the post of Professor of Divinity at St. Andrews University.

In 1911, the Rev. Neil Hugh MacColl submitted to the Church of Scotland's Colonial Committee a report of a visit he had made to Patagonia and the Falkland Islands. Thereafter, the Church of Scotland, in conjunction with the United Free Church, made strenuous efforts to involve itself in the life of Patagonia.

By the 1920s, when the Church of Scotland committed to sending itinerating minsters into the area, the vast distances involved between the estancias meant that the services continued to be mainly held irregularly and within the family homes.

The Rev. James Taylor, an Assistant Minister at the Belgrano Church of Scotland in Buenos Aires, travelled by land and sea during the latter part of the 1920s to visit the many families scattered across the sheep farms of Patagonia, but considerable time could elapse between ministers being either able or willing to take on the task.[2]

Neil Hugh MacColl was born in Mull in 1883, son of Angus MacColl and Margret McLennan. He was ordained as a chaplain in Argentina on 8 March 1908. Appointed to Patagonia in 1912, but after illness forced him to abandon Patagonia, he returned to Buenos Aires where he served until 1926.[3]

The Rev. MacColl had travelled originally to Patagonia on a mission of inquiry. On completion of his trip he was able to furnish the Church of Scotland with a significant assessment of the need for, and the conditions required of, a Patagonian Mission. Because of the scattered nature of the population, the work would involve visiting various estancias and serving religious needs in small groups. There would be little or no opportunity for addressing large congregations. However, he was confident that a minister would be made very welcome and the work had the potential of being very rewarding. The Rev. MacColl warned not to expect significant results in the short term, and that success: 'would not be measured by numbers alone, but by the changes in human character and behaviour'.

The Rev. MacColl found it difficult to put a number on the likely scattered congregation, but he believed that the number of Scots in Patagonia at the time ran into thousands, and due to the geographic extent of the region the minister would have his work cut out to get around everyone. Secular, as well as religious, instruction would need to be on the agenda and not just for the children:

> *Religious observances and practices will have to be re-established in many a household, young men will have to be encouraged to walk in the path of duty, and the erring and the lost will have to be re-claimed.*[4]

Additionally the climate, especially in winter, was described as 'rigorous'.

The Rev. MacColl finally describes the type of person that would be best suited to the job of Patagonian minister:

> *He will require to be a thoroughly sane and honest man, he must be possessed of infinite tact and of a strong sense of right and wrong. He must be hard working and own an inexhaustible store of patience, for he will have to probably wait long for the fruits of his toil.*[5]

The Church of Scotland's intent on serving Patagonia was reinforced at the next meeting of its Colonial Committee, when it was decided that the annual salary should be raised to £400 and a notice placed in *Life and Work* seeking a minister as soon as possible. Given the Rev. MacColl's existing knowledge of the area and to give the Church time to find a permanent minister it was agreed that the Rev. MacColl should be offered a one-year contract. Although this was a new mission, the Church did not feel overly concerned about its prospects, given that they anticipated that it would be well supported by people who would have largely been brought up in the Faith.

In 1912, the Rev. MacColl set out once again for Patagonia. At first all seemed to be going well. The Buenos Aires Scotch Church Magazine for February reported on the Rev. MacColl's mission. It recorded the baptisms and marriages performed by him and noted that a school at San Julián was among his plans. With regards to the financial maintenance of such a mission it was expected to be largely self-supporting and he had arranged for a 'Mr J Fraget to act as Treasurer at San Julián and Mr James Slater at Gallegos'.[6]

Alas, during 1914, the Rev. MacColl was forced to return to Scotland due to ill health. The climate had been severe, and the long distances he had had to travel had begun to tell on his none-too-robust health.

During his time in Patagonia the Rev. MacColl came into contact with, and was well known to, the Caithness Patagonian John Hamilton. In 1914 the Church decided to write to John Hamilton at Punta Loyola to elicit his views on the ministerial work required and on the extent to which the Church might expect to receive subscriptions.

Hamilton sent a letter to the Church Committee dated 8 December 1914. What it said is not known – but the committee decided to put the post on hold. The outbreak of war and possible shortage of Church funds may have been causes of the postponement.

By 1923 the situation was still not resolved, and the Church was again looking for a solution to supporting what they claimed were 20,000 people of Scottish parentage in Patagonia. Efforts were also being made to try and work in conjunction with the United Free Church. By early 1924 the two churches finally agreed that the Rev. Douglas W. Bruce should make a six-month visit to Patagonia, with plans to sail from Scotland at the end of September.

The Rev. Bruce, born 1 June 1885, was a man of some experience. Educated at Banff and Fordyce Academies, he went on to gain a Master of Arts at Aberdeen University. He was licensed by the Presbytery of Fordyce in 1910, became an Assistant at Buenos Aires before returning to Edinburgh's St. Cuthbert's as an assistant in 1912. The Rev. Bruce served as a combatant in France during the First World War. In 1915 he was ordained to Cadzow before being transmitted as minister of St. Stephens, Broughty Ferry. By 1926 he was back in Buenos Aires, and became president of the St. Andrew's Society of the River Plate in 1933/34; in 1939 he became a Doctor of Divinity.

By June 1925, the Rev. Bruce was back in Scotland, delivering a full and informative report to the General Assembly, which was subsequently printed in the Church's *Life and Work* journal. The Rev. Bruce reckoned he had covered some 3,650 miles across Patagonia by both car and on horseback, where he sought to minister to some 3,000 people of Scottish extraction 'all dependent on the humble sheep'.[7]

The Rev. Bruce baptised 57 children in Patagonia; among them was Jessie MacGregor Bain, either the daughter of Caithness couple Donald Bain and Helen (née Ross) or of Donald's brother William Bain and his Caithness wife, Elizabeth (née Sinclair). Both of these couples had daughters named Jessie MacGregor Bain after their Caithness grandmother, Jessie Bain (née MacGregor).

For some children the sight of this new man with, as he put it, 'a collar that buttons ahint', was too much. The Rev. Bruce relates how at one shepherd's farm the children hid in the bushes while their mother tried – and failed – to catch them. Dad, however, used his lasso to rope them in. The use of the lasso was primarily for the capturing of sheep, and Caithness Patagonian pioneer Andrew Harper was something of an expert. His descendants tell of how, after he returned from Patagonia, he would demonstrate his expertise on his farm near Thrumster in Caithness.

The people of Patagonia were quite isolated, with often 50 miles between neighbours. The art of any conversation, let alone religious conversation, was scanty. The Rev. Bruce was informed by one of our Caithness Patagonians that apart from little opportunity for conversation there was no time for talk beyond sheep matters: 'Padre, the fourth commandment here is "Six days thou shall labour and on the seventh thou shall gather sheep".'[8]

The hospitality of the congregation, however, was warming. Because the farms were so far apart there was no way of informing families in advance when the minister might arrive – he simply turned up. Yet there was always a bed and food, and in many a case the minister would be told that his was the first 'blessing of food' in that home. This hospitality continues today; visitors are made most welcome by the residents, who willingly open up their homes to travellers.

The necessity for the Patagonian minister to cover these vast distances meant that the Church provided a car, and for the Rev. Bruce to conduct his Patagonian mission the Church agreed to increase his allowance to compensate for the acquisition and running of the vehicle. The Rev. Bruce however found that, again due to the distances and the terrain, things did not always run smoothly:

> On one occasion two pet ostriches had followed us from an estancia and were greatly interested in a break-down we experienced. Their interest had been greatly material for we soon discovered that they had swallowed three important screws-nuts.[9]

The Rev. Bruce was in no doubt that Patagonia needed and wanted a minister, and based on his recommendations it was decided that an advertisement should be placed in the Scottish daily newspapers seeking to recruit a minister for Patagonia. In June 1925 the following appeared in *The Scotsman*:

Minister – C of S or U.F. minister wanted immediately for Patagonia, preferably under 35; three years engagement (renewable); part of each year in Buenos Aires; salary, £600; new motor car; £100 annually for expenses and first class return fare; unique opportunity for vigorous man. Applications, before July 4th, to Thomas Henderson, 22 Queen Street, Edinburgh.[10]

These conditions basically followed the Rev. Bruce's suggestions, but he did add one or two more 'suggestions':

- The car to be a self-starter Ford

- The minister to be of cheerful disposition, a good mixer with people, able to fend for himself, not too easily upset by a rough reception, ready to sleep where night finds him.
- It would be helpful if he could play the piano and sing
- The tour of the Camps should be from Punta Arenas to Última Esperanza and then to Punta Deseado and be conducted between October and April. Plus a month in Tierra del Fuego every second year.
- A printed receipt book should be carried to receipt any subscriptions received (the annual subscriptions in 1925 were estimated at c. £1000).
- All baptisms, marriages etc. to be registered in St. Andrew's Buenos Aires.

Two applications for the post were received. One from the Rev. James Marshall, BD, Church of Scotland Minister at Rosyth, and the second from the Rev. Murdo Macleod, assistant at St. Paul's Parish Church, Leith. The Rev. Marshall was subsequently appointed, with a start date of October 1925. His tenure, however ,did not last long; by June 1926 he had resigned and was heading for home because of ill health. He was diagnosed as suffering from neurasthenia.

The Rev. George D. Hutton, a previous convener of the Colonial Committee of the Church of Scotland, reported that on a visit to Punta Arenas in 1927 he had met with some of the subscribers to the Patagonian Scots Chaplaincy Fund, but again in 1927 the Church resolved not to make a Patagonian appointment but asked if Buenos Aires could spare someone to make a visit. The reply suggested that if the Colonial Committee would meet the costs, then an assistant could have half of his time allocated to Patagonia. Come July 1928 it was decided that the Rev. James S. Taylor would fulfil this task.

In 1929, St Andrew's Kirk Session, Buenos Aires, intimated that they could not support another trip to Patagonia at this time, but suggested that Mr James MacIntyre, whose term at Bahia Blanca was coming to an end, would be willing to go to and visit Patagonia. In 1931, St Andrew's Church Buenos Aires was again able to release an assistant – Mr George Buchanan – for Patagonia. Mr Buchanan went to Patagonia in 1932.

The register of births and baptisms for St Andrew's Presbyterian Church, Buenos Aires, includes an entry for James Peter Nicol, son of Caithness couple Alexander Nicol and Janet (née Nicolson), baptised by the Rev. MacColl. Bobby Bain, son of Angus Robert Bain and born in Patagonia in 1933, was baptised by the Rev. Bruce. The practice continued into more recent times – a current descendant tells us that she was baptised at Estancia Josefina in 1966.

Naturally in such a widespread district, the services of a minister were rarely more than a yearly or half-yearly event. Irrespective of the family's preferred faith, children were baptised and couples married by either the Church of Scotland or Anglican ministers, whoever appeared at the appropriate time.

1 As retold by Donald MacDonald.

2 *The Scotsman* 17 May 1929.

3 *Fasti Ecclesiae Scoticanae: The Succession of Ministers in the Church of Scotland from the Reformation.* - https://archive.org/details/fastiecclesiaesc00scot

4 *Life and Work*: the magazine of the Church of Scotland. 1911.

5 *Life and Work*: the magazine of the Church of Scotland. 1911.

6 *Life and Work*: the magazine of the Church of Scotland. 1913.

7 *Life and Work*: the magazine of the Church of Scotland. 1925.

8 *Life and Work*: the magazine of the Church of Scotland. 1925.

9 *Life and Work*: the magazine of the Church of Scotland. 1925.

10 *The Scotsman*, 17 June 1925.

Economic Life

Patagonia was not one of the Argentine government's public service priorities, yet in the late 19th and early 20th centuries it was a rapidly developing area. The basis for its development and growth was agricultural. The industrial needs and infrastructures needed to support the sheep farming industry naturally followed. While many Scots led the way in developing its agriculture, Scotland was also the source for engineers and engineering. The Glasgow-based company Kincaid and Co. built a relatively unique all-steel paddle steamer on the Clyde for trading use on the Rio Negro in Patagonia.

As towns like Rio Gallegas grew, so did the essential and ceremonial public service departments. Yet in 1947 the streets of Rio Gallegas were still not paved.

To this day in Caithness we find organisations such as the lifeboats and fire services being manned by volunteers. Volunteering was no less important in Patagonia. In the early days there were often few or significant 'professional' numbers of people. The police, where they existed, found it difficult to cover the vast areas. They were arranged into three geographic groups – north, south and the mountainous areas, with bases in Rio Gallegos, Deseado and Lake St. Martin. Further police out-stations were spread across the territory. Dealing with an issue or investigating a complaint could take the policeman away from his base for days, leaving the police station, if not unattended, then in the control of a subordinate. The Patagonian Gendarmeria seem to have been less than competent, and the British Consul in 1922 considered that they displayed: 'gross behaviour and undisciplined habits'.[1]

When it came to providing firemen, communities relied on the willingness and goodwill of local inhabitants. Punta Arenas relied on a Volunteer Fire Department, manned by people of various nationalities, backed by fire engines and appliances, which the British Consul noted in 1922, were of British make.[2] At the Frigorifico Bories all staff were trained as fire fighters, with regular fire drills carried out. The economic consequence of fire at these refrigeration plants was not just a halt in production, but the potential loss of animals, both live and slaughtered.

Communication in the camp was difficult, mainly because of the great distances that had to be travelled, and smoke signals were sometimes used by shepherds to communicate their positions when rounding up sheep. The roads were at best poor, and often non-existent. Where they did exist they were mainly for the use of the estancias. As one report pointed out: 'where convenience for the rancher ends, so there ends the road'.[3]

As to the construction of the roads, they were initially the result of tracks made by the carts. The early settlers were also responsible for building the necessary bridges. Yet people and goods had to be transported. Carts pulled by up to ten horses or mules would convey the larger loads. Passenger traffic tended to be by buckboard cart pulled by three horses with a fresh group of horses driven alongside.[4]

Road building did however get under way in some parts of Patagonia. In 1909 the Liverpool building firm J. H. & W Bell was awarded a contract to construct two miles of road and a 360-foot span bridge over the River Gallegas. The men and the plant were shipped from Britain along with all the necessary timber – there were few trees in Patagonia.[5] Whether Caithness pioneer Angus MacPherson planted trees or just simply wished for their existence is now difficult to assess, but in the drawings he included in his diaries, he pictured trees around the farm.

Today the main coastal highways in Patagonia are 'paved', and there is a programme to pave more of the roads that link the internal areas. It is a long and arduous process, given the costs involved and the extent of the land to cover. So many routes in Patagonia continue as gravel roads.

Railways have long proven to be a key element in the development of a region's economy. A debate over railways being built across Patagonia began, and was centred around who had the right to the land. Much of Patagonia had in effect been sold at very low prices to the farming fraternity, so to build railways meant having to buy back some of this land. Not the most popular decision for a government that was strapped for cash and that was in reality little interested in the development of Patagonia.

A narrow-gauge railway began construction in 1909 between Puerto Deseado and Las Heras, for the transportation of wool. Its function remained largely commercial and never really contributed to enable the opening-up of the area.

By the 1930s an air service had been established in Rio Gallegas; initially it could take some 12 hours from Buenos Aires to Rio Gallegas. Ships also plied from Buenos Aires to the towns along the coast with passengers and goods.

Apart from the coalmines still at Rio Turbio, it is difficult now to recognise that Patagonia once had over 100 locations where coal and lignite were found. They reached their peaks during the two world wars, when Argentina was very short of fuel.[6]

Samuel Morse in the United States of America demonstrated the first overland telegraph message in1844. Telephone lines were put into place connecting Punta Arenas, Última Esperanza and Rio Gallegas in 1900, and the transPatagonian telegraph line was completed in 1903. Even today, Caithness people are only too well aware of the ravages the winter weather can wreak on their power lines. But in Patagonia, where these lines covered many miles of vast spaces, finding and fixing the faults was a very difficult task. In the early days of the telephone in Puerto San Julián there were 70 subscribers in the town and only 10 in the camp. Not unusual in Patagonia, as in many far-flung areas of the world at the time, was the fact that the system ran as a party line, so that the other subscribers on the line could listen in if they chose.

Today, oil production is key to economic success in Argentina. Comodora Rividavia in the north-east of Patagonia hosts the area's major oil production. Here, oil wells are producing some 15,000 litres per day.

1 British Consul's Tour of Patagonia (1922).
2 British Consul's Tour of Patagonia (1922).
3 *La Patagonia Argentina*.
4 *The Scotsman* 4 January 1916.
5 *Daily Mail* 9 October 1909.
6 http://www.railwaysofthefarsouth.co.uk/09athecoalfield.html.

PART II
The Pioneers

Caithness men and women were among the many Scots who emigrated to and conquered the wild lands of Patagonia. Some of their experiences and contributions have been told in the above chapters. Many of them made their homes in Patagonia, yet their current descendants continue to hold a special place for Caithness in their hearts and minds. Their family histories and the places where their ancestors lived and grew up are important links to their heritage. Connections to current relatives are also important, for many of those relatives that continue to live in Caithness and beyond also feel a pride in their pioneering ancestors. Links between 'cousins' in Caithness and Patagonia are in many cases strong, and are nurtured through visits and the power of social media.

To help identify and understand the origins of those Caithness Patagonian Pioneers, extensive research has been conducted in tracing their origins. While some of this has been enabled through public records, it is the help, support and enthusiasm of the current generations that have made it possible. The following biographical sketches aims to help place the Caithness roots of those Patagonian Pioneers and to celebrate and acknowledge the extent of the challenges these Caithness men and women took on and conquered.

The current research has identified the following Caithness men and women who have played a role in the development of Patagonia:

Angus Robert Bain: David Bain: Donald Bain: George Bain: Jessie Lizzie Bain: Rebecca Sinclair Bain: William Bain: David Barnetson: William Begg: Sinclair Bremner: Annie Budge: William Budge: Annie Chapman: David Christian: Donald Christian: Henry Christian: Ben Gunn Cormack: Jessie Cormack: John Cormack: James Earsman: Percy Earsman: (William Earsman): John Hamilton: Andrew Harper: John Harper: Robert Harper: George Hendry: James Hendry: John Hendry: William Hendry: Alexander MacDonald: Robert MacDonald: (Donald MacKay): Helen MacKay: James MacKay: Jean MacKay: Alexander McKenzie: William McKenzie: John McKinnon: Charlotte MacLean: John MacLeod: Angus McPherson: Hugh McPherson: Lucy Miller: Christina Mowat: John Cormack Mowat: John Munro: Alexander Nicol: Alexander Nicolson: Donald Nicolson: Janet Nicolson: Robert Nicolson: John Oman: Nicol Oman: Alexander Plowman: George Plowman: James Plowman: Helen Ross: William Sutherland Ross: Elizabeth Sinclair: John Hymers Sutherland: Sinclair Sutherland: Williamina Sutherland.

From Rags to Riches

The Caithness Patagonian Pioneers left a number of legacies: current generations of the Bain family continue to be significant Patagonian sheep farmers; a school in Perito Merino is the product of Angus McPherson's generosity; descendants of the Earsmans, Nicolsons and Barnetsons play key roles in Argentinian public life. Fond memories are retained of the characters such as George Plowman and Alexander MacKenzie, and connections between members of the Oman family have been re-kindled.

The Hamilton legacy is evident in Patagonia and Caithness. A street in Rio Gallegas bearing his name marks John Hamilton's contribution to the development of sheep farming in Patagonia. His entrepreneurial sheep farming and business skills formed the basis of his great-grandsons' continuing sheep farming success. But despite his Patagonian success, he never forgot his native Caithness: the John Hamilton Trust was established to provide financial support for Caithness farms and businesses.

John Hamilton was the son of a clothier in Wick. Born on 15 March 1858, he was the third of nine children. His father, Angus Hamilton, was the owner of Hamilton & Co. Clothiers based at 52 Dempster Street, Wick. His mother was Catherine, daughter of Donald Sutherland, farmer at Flex in Watten, and his wife Barbara (née Craig).

Angus Hamilton had been born in Wick c. 1824, the son of Alexander Hamilton and Elizabeth Weir. On 3 March 1854 Angus Hamilton married Catherine (Kate) Sutherland, and by 1861 he was established in Wick as a tailor employing two men. His home was in Janetstown, Wick, but by 1871 the family had moved to East Banks in Wick. He continued to live there until his death on 3 June 1903.

It was not uncommon in the mid to late 19th century for families to be large in number. Angus and Catherine Hamilton had nine children, yet they were unlikely to be among the poorest families in Wick.

In 1880, at the relatively young age of 22, John Hamilton decided to leave home for a shepherding life on the opposite side of the world. Going abroad was not uncommon – but he was a clothier's son, so why as a shepherd? His grandfather on his mother's side was a farmer, not far from Wick, at Flex near Watten. There may also have been a latent farming gene from John's other grandfather, a crofter in the hills behind Brora in Sutherland.

By that time, world travel and emigration was not uncommon, and Caithness people were among those who settled in various far-flung places. John Hamilton was somewhat different in that he chose the South American continent rather than the normal Empire destinations of Canada or Australia. His initial destination, however, was the British colony of the Falkland Islands.

The Falkland Islands Company actively recruited Scots to work their sheep farms, and John was not the first from Caithness to make the journey; James Nicol from Clashach near Halkirk had already made it to the Falkland Islands in 1879. Why John chose the Falklands remains unclear. No known connection existed between him and James Nicol, but Caithness is a relatively small place and word of mouth has always been a key means of communication.[1]

Two other Hamilton brothers also went abroad: John's brother William emigrated to Australia sometime after 1881 and Daniel became the proprietor of a dry goods store in Needham, Norfolk, in Massachusetts, USA. He had been born 22 July 1856 in Wick, and married Johanna Gunn from Buckie on 8 June 1883; until his emigration in 1888, he had worked in the family firm as a drapery manager. John always willingly supported his family financially, and when Daniel's business hit some difficult times, John came to his rescue. Another brother, Francis, born 11 February 1868, made his way to London.

The sons and daughters of many large families were under some pressure to seek their future by going abroad. The large Hamilton family, like many others, was also at the mercy of children dying young.

Andrew Key Hamilton died aged two on 19 November 1872, as a result of contracting scarlatina, and is buried in Watten Cemetery alongside his maternal grandparents, Donald and Barbara (née Craig) Sutherland. John's sister, Barbara, lived a relatively short life; born 19 March 1860, she lived in the family home at East Banks, Wick, until her death there on 31 July 1895. John's eldest brother, Alexander, was born in 1855. He followed his father's trade of tailoring, and also lived at the family home in East Banks. Along with another daughter, Elizabeth, and indeed a considerable number of people from Caithness (including another Caithness Patagonian), Alexander ended his days at Sunnyside Hospital in Montrose. He died there on 30 November 1913. Elizabeth died there on 3 May 1915.

Another of John's brothers, James, born 23 December 1866, was the eventual heir to the Hamilton clothier business and, in partnership with John, handled some of John's Patagonian business in Wick. John was also to retain the services of Caithness firm Georgeson & Sons as his legal representative.

James Hamilton married twice. Firstly he married Christina Couper, a farmer's daughter from Hempriggs near Wick. After her death, he married Catherine Weir, on 25 October 1895. The Hamilton connection with the Forss area of Caithness began when James moved to the farm Burn of Brims. By 1928/29 James is listed in the Caithness Valuation Roll as proprietor of the farm. He died at Forss Schoolhouse on 30 November 1944, where his daughter Catherine was the teacher.

John Hamilton left Wick in 1880, reputedly with £5 from his mother's kist.[2] This however was no madcap financial gamble; John had signed a five-year contract with the London-based Falkland Islands Company; similar contracts of the time offered wages of up to £60 by the end of the agreed period. The company had launched a sheep-rearing business across 500,000 hectares of land that it had acquired in the islands. The population of the Falkland Islands at the time of John Hamilton's arrival was just under 1,500.

The Falkland Islands sheep farming industry had effectively begun in 1852 with the formation in London of the Falkland Islands Company. It first introduced Cheviot sheep to the islands, and by the 1860s there was a significant increase in sheep farming.

At the expiry of John Hamilton's initial Falkland Islands contract in 1885 he, like a number of others, realised that there was little opportunity of acquiring his own land on the Falklands; most of the available land was already saturated with sheep, and mainly owned by the Falkland Islands Company. So John looked across to mainland Patagonia, and sailed to Oazy Harbour, northeast of Punta Arenas in Chile.

His decision to head for Patagonia coincided with Carlos Maria Moyano, the governor of Patagonia's Santa Cruz province, making a trip to the Falkland Islands, with the express purpose of persuading shepherds to move from the Falklands to Patagonia. Moyano bought around 600 sheep and convinced 15 shepherds to make the move.[3]

In 1889 John, with Thomas Saunders, another entrepreneurial Scottish emigrant, formed a partnership that established estancias in the region of Rio Gallegas in Patagonia. The company, Hamilton & Saunders, commenced with 22 leagues[4] purchased at a cost of $1,200 gold pesos per league.

One report claimed that in

> 1893 their business sheared 42000 sheep and they owned 58 square leagues of land, of which 20 leagues were paid in full and the mortgage on the rest was in such shape as to give them no uneasiness … the sale of wool from these 42000 sheep earned them $42000 gold clean profit, above all expenses.[5]

Another report from the same period highlighted that 500 hoggets[6] were sold at $7.50 each, and when they were dressed they weighed in at 75 lbs.[7]

Thomas Saunders, originally from Fife (along with his brother William) also arrived in Patagonia from the Falkland Islands. Thomas built his first house with his own bare hands at Otway Station, and today his tomb stands there in remembrance.

> The firm of Hamilton and Saunders was one of the most renowned in Argentina as well as in Chilian [sic] Patagonia, and its stockbreeding establishments were models as far as plant and methods of administration are concerned.[8]

The Patagonian town of Rio Gallegas recognised the impact that John Hamilton had had on the development of the region, and named a street Calle Juan Hamilton in his honour.

On the death of Thomas Saunders there ensued a long-drawn-out legal process of settling the resulting breakup of the company. Eventually John transferred much of his personal share in Hamilton & Saunders Ltd into the company John Hamilton Ltd, thereby removing himself from personal liability.

Long before that, however, in 1888, John Hamilton, Thomas Saunders, Henry Jamieson, John McLean and George McGeorge[9] had embarked on a two-year trek, herding a vast quantity of sheep and horses some 2,000 miles across Argentina. The expedition was to help stock the estancias of the five sheep farmers, and at the end of the journey each of the partners had about 2,000 sheep. The journey is now legendary not just because of its magnitude, but because of the relative inexperience of the five leading shepherds. (A fuller account of the trek is given in the chapter 'Sheep.')

John Hamilton became an accomplished horseman and is credited as a 'horse whisperer'. In a land where the horse was the main means of transport, it was also a potential lifesaver and companion across the vast distances, so this was a skill worth its weight. Whether or not John was a horse whisperer he would certainly have learned many of his horsemanship skills from the native people. They were skilled horsemen, and John is known to have built up good relations with the indigenous Patagonians.

As his business grew, John was instrumental in encouraging other Caithness men to come to Patagonia. The *John O'Groat Journal* of 21 April 1891 printed the following advertisement:

Wanted Shepherds – a few single young men for Patagonia, South America. Five years engagement, wages £30 first year, rising to £60 last year. Passage paid out and home and keep found during whole tenure of engagement. Apply personally by letter to James Hamilton, Clothier, 52 Dempster Street, Pulteneytown, Wick.

A mere six months later the *John O'Groat Journal* was carrying a similar advertisement. This time the starting wage being offered had risen to £50:

Wanted Shepherds – a few single young men for Patagonia, South America. Five years engagement, wages £50 first year, rising to £60 last year. Passage paid out and home and keep found during whole tenure of engagement. Apply immediately, personally or by letter to James Hamilton, Clothier, 52 Dempster Street, Pulteneytown, Wick.[10]

This was surely a significant inducement to join the Patagonian sheep industry. When compared with other advertisements of the time, such as 'House Tablemaid in New Brunswick – £24 + passage (2nd Class)' or 'Teacher, Helmsdale Public School – £35', Hamilton's offer must have looked very attractive.

John Hamilton made his home in Patagonia, where he married, and raised a family of two daughters. His wife Olivia was the daughter of Richard Heap, a cotton mill mechanic in Glasgow, and his wife Olive (née Smith), to whom Olivia had been born at 109 Castle Street, Glasgow, on 12 August 1865. The Heap family came originally from Lancashire, that other great cotton mill region. Olivia and John met and married in Argentina in 1903 while she was working as a nurse at the British Hospital in Buenos Aires. She had originally sailed to Argentina from Liverpool on 14 March 1895, along with her brother Arthur.

Two daughters were born to John and Olivia Hamilton. The elder, Olive Sutherland, was born in 1906 in Punta Arenas[11] and went on to marry Alexander MacKay Gallie, originally from Tain, on 27 April 1929.

The younger, Penelope, was born 3 February 1910 in Argentina, and lived there until her death on 24 May 1986. Both Olive and Penelope were educated in Scotland; in the early 1920s the girls were enrolled at Lansdowne House School in Edinburgh. (Today the school remains one of the few all-girls schools in Scotland and currently operates under the name of St. George's School for Girls.)

John and Olivia made regular trips to Britain to visit the girls, although much of the day-to-day administration of the girls' time at school was in the hands of John's solicitors, Georgeson & Son in Wick. Olive returned to Patagonia in 1927 and Penelope in 1931.

Prior to Olive's untimely death in 1936, she made at least two trips to Britain with her husband, Alexander MacKay Gallie. In 1929 they sailed to London on the *Andes*, and again in 1934, this time accompanied by their son Andrew.

Penelope married into an Alvarez family and made her home in Argentina. Today the descendants of both daughters continue to farm the Hamilton lands in Patagonia.

Penelope died on 24 May 1986, and is buried in the Chacarita Cemetery in Buenos Aires alongside her father and mother. John Hamilton honoured Penelope when he named a boat after her; the *Penelope* was purchased in 1929 as a means of sailing between Argentina and the Falkland Islands. On John's death, Penelope inherited the boat and in 1952 gifted it to the British Services Antarctic Expedition, where it continued to be used to transport people, cattle and equipment from one island to another.[12]

John Hamilton kept in close contact with developments in the Falkland Islands, and began to acquire some properties on the islands. In 1922 he bought Beaver Island and some smaller adjacent isles from Richard Waldon Thornhill of Punta Arenas. Later he purchased more land there: Weddell Island, the Passage Islands and Saunders Island. He also owned property in the town of Stanley.

He also attempted to buy the Jason Islands but on that occasion was unsuccessful, as they belonged to the British Crown.

John's main base was in Argentina but he continued to play an active role in the development of the Falkland Islands, sharing his time between Argentina,

Britain and the Falklands. Weddell Island had been overgrazed so he initiated programmes of stock reduction, the replanting of the native tussac grass and the importing of coniferous seedlings from Punta Arenas; a legend says that John Hamilton took seeds from a gorse bush in Bower in Caithness and planted them in Patagonia.

In an attempt at diversification on his Falkland Island properties, John set up a seal oil production programme (not very successful), and introduced animals such as foxes, skunks, otters and guanacos for their pelts and skins. He also introduced Shetland ponies and Highland cattle onto his Falklands properties.

His first consignment of ponies came from Scotland, but had to be destroyed on arrival, following an outbreak of anthrax on the ship. Later shipments of Shetland ponies were delivered, but John was unable to personally supervise the purchase of them, and questioned the pedigree of the stock.

Foxes were the plague of sheep farmers and given that the original Falklands foxes had been declared extinct in 1876, their introduction seemed a strange decision by John, himself a sheep farmer.

The guanaco industry never really flourished (although many remain on Staats Island in the Falklands). The Highland cattle and Shetland pony experiments only lasted while John was alive and took an interest in them.

He donated funds to build lighthouses on East and West Falkland, and made a contribution towards the costs of improvements to the King Edward VII Memorial Hospital.[13]

He was an advocate of road building and encouraged research into a project in the camp. In December 1940 ownership of the properties on the Falkland Islands was transferred to John Hamilton Estates Ltd.[14]

But he never forgot his homeland of Caithness. He established a trust fund that was designed to help develop farms and businesses in Caithness. Many benefited from this fund over the years.

We know that John Hamilton made a number of trips back to Britain. The earliest recorded trip was in May 1910 when he travelled first class on board the *Amazon* from Buenos Aires to Southampton. In 1922 he sailed with his wife Olivia and daughters Olive and Penelope from Punta Arenas to Liverpool on board the *Ortega*, giving an onward destination as c/o James Hamilton (his brother), Wick. In 1925, with only his wife Olivia on this occasion, he sailed from La Plata to London on the *Highland Loch* with an onward destination of the Norfolk Hotel, London. July 1927 found him with his wife and daughter Olive, again travelling first class, on the *Orania*, again with an onward address of the Norfolk Hotel, London. In June 1937 John and Olivia were on board the *Clement* from Buenos Aires to Liverpool, with a listed address of c/o J. Hoare & Co., 19 London Wall.

John retained an interest in and communication with his family in Caithness. In 1931, by which time he was firmly established at Punta Loyola, Rio Gallegos, he wrote to his nephew, Frank Hamilton, at Burn of Brims, Forss in Caithness. The letter recounts some of his Falkland Island experiences. He wrote again in 1933, this time to his brother James with some veiled comments about money matters; John had earlier purchased the family house in East Banks, where his parents lived.

In later life John developed a serious eye problem and in order to obtain regular treatment in Buenos Aires, he bought and moved to a stud farm at Merlo, west of the city. His wife Olivia died in October 1942. John lived on until September 1945. His daughter, Penelope Alvarez, survived him.

John Hamilton died a highly respected man:

An indefatigable worker, it may be said of him, that from the time he settled he never had a moment's repose, and even now, old as he is, his activity belies the testimony which his snowy hair gives of his years.[15]

---

1 James Nicol's story is beyond the scope of this work, as he was eventually to settle in Canada as opposed to Patagonia.
2 Strongbox.
3 *Argentina's Rise: The Falkland Islands* - https://falklandstimeline.wordpress.com/1850-1899/
4 A traditional Spanish measure of area, equivalent to about 4 acres or 1.8 hectares.
5 *The Gold Diggings of Cape Horn/* John R. Spears. 2012.
6 Yearlings – not yet old enough to have been sheared for the first time.
7 Thomas Fenton: letter to his mother.
8 *La Patagonia Argentina.*
9 *From the Falklands to Patagonia/* Michael James Mainwaring. Alison & Busby. 1983.
10 *The John O'Groat Journal*, 4 August 1891.
11 St James Baptisms.
12 Libro Malvinas.
13 *Dictionary of Falklands Biography/* David Tatham, 2008.
14 *The Enigma of Guanacos in the Falkland Islands; the legacy of John Hamilton/* William L. Franklin and Melissa M. Grigione in Journal of Biogeography (2005) 32. 661–675.
15 http://patlibros.org/lpa/vwset/hamilton.htm

Brothers and Sisters

William Bain, crofter and fisherman from Mavesy near Lybster in Caithness and his wife Jessie (née MacGregor) had a family of seven sons and four daughters. Five of the sons and two of the daughters left Caithness for Patagonia during the late 19th and early 20th centuries. The brothers all returned to Caithness for wives. Two of these wives were themselves sisters. The daughter and son of one of the two Bain sisters who remained at home also made their way to join the Bain enterprises in Patagonia. The daughter of one of the Patagonian Bain brothers married the nephew of the Caithness Patagonian Nicolson brothers, originally from Clyth.

Sadly, two sons of William and Jessie Bain died very young; the two boys, Robert and Angus, both died in 1887 victims of a measles epidemic that spread across Caithness. There can be little doubt that life on the small croft in Mavesy would at the very best have been crowded, so maybe it is little surprise that William would have sought opportunities elsewhere.

William Bain, born on 26 April 1877, was the eldest of the surviving sons of William Bain and Jessie (née MacGregor). William senior had been born in 1846, and Jessie MacGregor in 1855.

William junior first settled in Patagonia in 1896 and gained employment from the sheep farming entrepreneur Mauricio Braun. By 1905 William was manager of the Braun firm's Estancia Josefina, which he ultimately purchased. Today his descendants continue to live at and work Estancia Josefina.

William was a visitor to the British Club in Punta Arenas in 1907; potentially this could have been conducting Braun business. He was back in Punta Arenas doing business with Mauricio Braun at the British Club in Punta Arenas in 1914. He again visited the club in 1925.

On 13 September 1910 he set a trend for his brothers, as he returned to Caithness to marry a local lass, Elizabeth Sinclair.

Elizabeth Sinclair was born on 15 December 1884 at Kirkhill, Halkirk. She was the daughter of Angus and Barbara Sinclair. Her sister, Donaldina Sinclair, who was also to make the trip to Patagonia, was also born in Halkirk, in 1888. Elizabeth and Donaldina lived at the family home of West Calder at the time of the 1891 census. By the time of the 1901 census, Elizabeth was working as a servant in the home of John Clyne at Dalmore, but Donaldina had moved with the rest of the family to Norland, Latheron, on the south-east coast of Caithness.

On 22 September 1910 William Bain junior, along with his new wife Elizabeth, set sail to return to Patagonia. Two years later she returned to her family home at Burnside, Reisgill, to give birth to a daughter, Jessie, born 3 November 1912. Elizabeth returned to Patagonia along with her sister-in-law Rebecca Bain on 27 February 1913 – but her baby, Jessie, seems not to have made the trip until April 1913.

Also in 1913 William, along with his brothers, Angus Robert, George and Donald, were founder members of the Sociedad Rural (Puerto Deseado Rural Society), a key organisation in the development and trade of the sheep farming industry in Patagonia.

In 1920 **James Sinclair**, a brother of Elizabeth Sinclair, travelled to Patagonia, then in May 1927 their sister **Donaldina Sinclair** returned from Patagonia to Lybster with the two daughters of Donald Bain, William's younger brother; the girls had been sent to live in Lybster and attend school there. Donaldina sailed back to Patagonia in October 1927 on the same ship as Caithness Patagonian Pioneer John Munro.

William, with his wife Elizabeth and daughter Jessie, made a trip to Caithness in June 1928. Jessie was now 15, and bearing in mind that she had been born in Lybster, this could have been a first, and hence emotional, return trip. Also on board the ship *Andes* was Clyth-born Robert Nicolson, on one of his regular trips from Patagonia to Caithness. The Bain family departed again for Buenos Aires from Southampton on 21 September 1928; David Bain (William's youngest brother) and his new wife Jessie, née Cormack, joined them on board.

William, Elizabeth and daughter Jessie returned again to Caithness in 1937, staying at the Portland Arms Hotel, Lybster, for the duration of their trip. This was William's last visit to his homeland, as he died on 9 July 1938. He is buried at Estancia Josefina.

Elizabeth continued to lead an active life into her old age. As the family matriarch, she spent the winter months in a Buenos Aires hotel, where she could be regularly found having tea with the grandchildren who attended school in the city. She is fondly remembered as someone who constantly bought gifts for family members, but when a birthday gift of a trip to Caithness was offered to her, she declined. She died on 7 October 1967.

Donald Bain, the second surviving son of William and Jessie Bain, was born on 5 October 1883 at Mavesy. By 1904 Donald had followed the family route to Patagonia and settled near Pico Truncado, where he founded a farm called Kolhuel Kaike. He made a return trip to Caithness in June 1911, and on 3 October 1911 he married Helen (Nellie) Ross at Wick Parish Church.

Helen Ross was born on 19 July 1884 at Achastle. Her father was Donald Ross, a merchant seaman and the owner of the boat *Willing Boys*, and her mother was Annie (née MacDonald) of Achastle. In 1901 Helen was working as a domestic servant in Tongue while Donald Bain at that time worked as a fisherman, living at the family home at Mavesy. Prior to her marriage to Donald Bain, Helen had acted as a witness at her sister Barbara's wedding; on 9 August 1907 Barbara Ross married Donald MacKay, a mason from Clyth.

Donald Bain was once more back in Caithness around 1912/1913. The purpose of this visit is not known, but he then returned to Patagonia again, sailing from Liverpool to Punta Arenas, in January 1913.

Tragedy struck Donald's family in January 1927 when his wife Helen died following the birth of their daughter, Elena. With young children to care for, he made the decision to send two of his daughters, Jessie MacGregor and Ameta, to their grandparents in Lybster, where they attended school. The children remained in Scotland until 1935.

Donald Bain died in 1954.

Angus Robert Bain, born 1887, and the third surviving son of William Bain and Jessie (née MacGregor), first departed for Patagonia in July 1908, travelling from Liverpool for Punta Arenas on board the *Orita*. He was joined on the journey by **Nicol Oman**, another Caithness Patagonian Pioneer.

Angus was back in Caithness in 1914 to visit friends and relatives. He returned to Patagonia along with Donald Nicolson from Clyth, on 1 October 1914. Angus Robert's profession at the time was stated as a carpenter, yet it was farming that had brought him to Patagonia; in 1918 he founded the successful farm called Tipperary.

He returned again to Caithness; on this occasion he arrived at Liverpool on 20 April 1924 and travelled north to the family home at Mavesy. This must have been an emotional return, as his mother had died in 1920. There is no evidence to suggest that any of the Patagonian children were at home at the time of her death. However, all was not sad. Angus Robert returned to Patagonia on 3 October 1924 with **Jane MacKay**, sister of George Bain's wife, Helen (née MacKay), as his companion. Jane initially went to live with her sister on Estancia Floradora, but Angus Robert and Jane must have got on well during the journey as the two were married on 30 April 1926 at Pico Truncado, Patagonia. Angus Robert and Jane settled in Patagonia where they brought up their family – a family that continues to grow, and plays a significant part in Argentinian life and culture.

Angus Robert died 15 December 1963 and is buried in Puerto Deseado.

George Bain, the eighth child of William and Jessie Bain, was born on 8 December 1889 at Mavesy. He was to become one of the Bain family members prominent in the development of sheep farming in Patagonia. He was also, along with his three brothers, William, Angus Robert and Donald, a founder member of the Sociedad Rural, Puerto Deseado, in 1913.

George initially left Caithness for Patagonia in August 1906, sailing from Liverpool to Punta Arenas. Also on board the *Orita* was his cousin and neighbour, George Hendry.

George Bain returned to Caithness, to marry Helen MacKay on 16 September 1920. The ceremony took place at the Berriedale Arms Inn in Mey. Helen had worked as a domestic servant at the Portland Arms Hotel in Lybster, so potentially the two had previously met in Lybster. The newly married couple sailed to Patagonia from Southampton on 24 September 1920. George's niece, Annie, accompanied them. But they could barely have reached Patagonia when news arrived of the death of George's mother, Jessie; she had died suddenly on 6 November 1920 at her home in Mavesy.

George became part-owner of Estancia Floradora, a significant Patagonian sheep farm, which to this day remains in the ownership of Bain descendants. George and Helen remained at Floradora until 1946, running the sheep farm and bringing up a family.

In May 1929 George and Helen, with son William and daughters Elizabeth, Jessie and Margaret, arrived back in Caithness, with a destination address of the MacKay family home in Mey. The family set sail again for Patagonia in September 1929, this time accompanied by Miss Christian Judge, a teacher from Avoch. She remained with the family for a few years, her remit being to teach the children at the home of George and Helen Bain.

In 1970 George and Helen celebrated their golden wedding in style, with a party at Estancia Floradora. Pipers had been flown in from Buenos Aires for the occasion, creating quite an emotional moment for the couple.

George died in Comodora Rivadavia on 19 September 1979, and Helen MacKay died 4 August 1982 at Estancia Floradora.

David Bain, the youngest of the sons of William Bain and Jessie (née MacGregor), was born at Mavesy on 1 September 1892. He enlisted in the Seaforth Highlanders in 1911 and served during the First World War. Following the war he joined his brothers in Patagonia and founded his farm, called Santa Elena. He too returned to Caithness for a wife; he arrived back in Lybster in June 1928, and on 17 September that year married Jessie Gunn Cormack, in Back Bridge Street, Wick. Another Caithness Patagonian pioneer, Robert Nicolson, was witness to the marriage.

Jessie Gunn Cormack was born on 27 August 1906 at Smerlie, the daughter of John Alexander Cormack and Elizabeth (née MacKenzie). Shortly after the wedding, on 21 September, the newly married couple sailed from Southampton for Patagonia, where they set up home and raised a family. In November 1933 David and Jessie Bain returned to Scotland, going firstly to the home of David's sister, Anne, in Carluke. David returned alone to Patagonia the following month, December 1933.

By April 1934 Jessie had returned to her family home at Smerlie, where she gave birth to a son, Donald Allan Cormack Bain. Tragically, three years later, on 30 June 1937, Jessie died at Sunnyside Hospital in Montrose.

David died in 1966, in Patagonia.

Rebecca Sinclair Bain was born on 5 October 1896 at Mavesy, the third daughter of William and Jessie Bain. The 1911 census records Rebecca as a visitor at the house of her sister, Anne Lightbody, in Carluke. In February 1913 Rebecca departed for Patagonia, along with her sister-in-law, Elizabeth Bain, William's wife. They travelled on 27 February 1913, destined for Buenos Aires.

Rebecca married Lachlan MacDonald on 2 February 1917 at the Hotel Argentino in Puerto Deseado. Lachlan was originally from Tiree, and probably arrived in Patagonia around 1906. The MacDonalds of Tiree were renowned pipers, and that piping tradition and skills continue within today's generation of Patagonian MacDonalds. Rebecca's daughter, Lola Rebecca MacDonald, re-energised the Caithness–Patagonian connection when she married **Alexander Nicolson**, originally from Clyth, on 26 April 1947. Alexander was the nephew of Robert and Donald Nicolson from Clyth, two of the original Caithness Patagonian Pioneers.

Rebecca Sinclair Bain died on 27 October 1973 and is buried in Puerto Deseado.

Jessie Lizzie Bain, the youngest of the Bain family, was born on 13 January 1895 at Mavesy. She left home on 3 September 1914 to join her brothers in Patagonia.

In 1917 Jessie Lizzie was bridesmaid at her sister Rebecca's marriage to Lachlan MacDonald, and then in 1919 in Puerto Deseado, she herself married Angus Shaw, originally from Lewis. Angus died on 22 April 1948 while Jessie Lizzie lived on until 23 November 1983 and is buried in Rio Gallegas.

Anne Bain, born 28 April 1875, was the eldest of the Bain children from Mavesy. She was the only one of all the brothers and sisters to have had no direct connection with Patagonia.

Anne continued to live in the family home at Mavesy until 1903, when she married Lybster fisherman William Munro on 4 December 1903. Sadly, William Munro died in the Edinburgh Infirmary on 17 November 1906, while resident at 32 Haymarket Terrace, Edinburgh.

By 1909 Anne had taken up the position of cook at The Manse in Roxburgh, when she re-married. Her second husband was Robert Lightbody, a widower, born in Cambusnethan in 1863, the son of a coal miner. Anne and Robert went on to raise a family and live the rest of their lives in Carluke.

Anne died 9 February 1945, at Canniesburn Hospital, Bearsden, in Glasgow.

Margaret Paterson Bain, second daughter of William Bain and Jessie (née MacGregor), was born 4 February 1879 in Lybster. Her husband, James Budge, was born on 4 May 1875 at Clyth.

In 1901 Margaret was employed as housekeeper by James Georgeson, a boot- and shoemaker in Lybster. James Budge at this time was working as a cooper and living with his family in Main Street, Lybster.

Margaret gave birth to a child, **Annie Bain**, on 13 July 1902 at the Bain home in Mavesy. But it was not until Margaret and James Budge got married, on 24 November 1905, that Annie was officially recognised as Annie Budge; in 1925 James Budge sought authority to correct the entry of her birth in the Register of Births to reflect him as her father.[1]

Annie started school in Lybster in May 1908 and continued to live at her grandparents' home in Mavesy. She left school in June 1917, and on 24 September 1920, departed for Patagonia, accompanied by her uncle George Bain and his wife Helen (née Campbell). Annie subsequently married Thomas O'Byrne at Estancia de San Julio, Puerto Deseado.

William Budge, son of Margaret (née Bain) and James Budge, was born on 7 December 1911, also at the Bain home in Mavesy. He started school in Lybster on 23 April 1917.

In September 1929 William followed the Patagonian route and worked for his uncle George Bain; William had travelled to Patagonia along with George and his family, plus George Plowman from Spittal. In 1936 William was appointed manager of an estancia owned by Colin Gordon, originally from the Black Isle in Scotland.

William returned to Britain in 1941 to join the wartime forces, and served as a sergeant in a tank regiment in Africa. Following the war, he chose not to return to Patagonia and in 1947 married Christina Adamson.

Margaret Budge died 1 February 1962 and is buried in Clyth. Her husband James died 4 October 1962. William died in 1997.

Not surprisingly, given that seven of the Bain family made their homes in Patagonia, the Bain name continues to thrive there today. As the five brothers all married ladies from Caithness, family connections also continue to have strong links with Caithness.

The Bain brothers and sisters made a significant imprint on sheep farming in Patagonia, and today third and fourth generations of Bains continue to live and work in Argentina.

---

1 National Archives of Scotland SC14/4B/1925/8.

The MacKay Sisters

The exodus from Caithness to Patagonia contained a number of family groups. Initially brothers followed brothers, before the men returned for Caithness wives. Among these were two Bain brothers, who married two sisters from Caithness. Helen and Jane MacKay from Lyth in Caithness united with the Bain family from Mavesy; Helen married George and Jane married Angus Robert.

The sisters were the daughters of William MacKay, blacksmith in Lyth, and Elizabeth Jane (née McAdie); William and Jane had married in Bower Parish on 1 October 1897. The family association with the blacksmith trade went back at least one generation; William MacKay's father, Donald MacKay, and William's brother, Alexander, had also been blacksmiths. Donald was tenant of two houses and land in Lyth until his death in 1904/1905. William became a tenant in his own right of a house with land at Todholes, Lyth, in 1907. Near neighbours were the family of John Earsman, whose sons, William, James and Percy, also went to Argentina. The MacKay family later moved to Mey in the north of Caithness, where William MacKay continued his blacksmith trade.

Helen Campbell MacKay was born at Lyth on 13 February 1900. Helen had set up home in Patagonia with George Bain following their marriage on 16 September 1920 in the Berriedale Arms Inn in Mey. Helen had been previously employed in the Portland Arms Hotel in Lybster, and presumably became acquainted with George Bain while he was in the village.

In May 1929, Helen, along with husband George, son William, and daughters Elizabeth, Jessie and Margaret, arrived back in Caithness to the MacKay family home in Mey. In September 1929 the family returned to Patagonia, this time accompanied by a teacher, Miss Christian Judge from Avoch; she took on the role of home tutor to the Bain children at Estancia Floradora.

In 1970 Helen and George Bain celebrated their golden wedding in style, with a party at the Sociedad Puerto Deseado.

Helen MacKay died on 4 August 1982.

Jane MacKay was born on 7 March 1906, also at Lyth. At the relatively young age of 18, she travelled from Southampton on 3 October 1924 to Patagonia, to be with her sister at Estancia Floradora. Her future husband, Angus Robert Bain, accompanied her on the boat journey. Jane and Angus Robert were married on 30 April 1926 at Pico Truncado, Patagonia, then went on to bring up their family in Patagonia. Their son, Bobby, is now the patriarch of the Patagonian Bain Clan. Jane never returned to Caithness.

Caithness Brides

The Caithness Patagonia story contains a number of Caithness women. Some of the Caithness Patagonian Pioneers returned to Caithness for wives. Others married prior to emigrating as couples. Donald MacKay was unique, however, in that he was born in Patagonia, the son of Caithness parents, then travelled to Caithness, married a Caithness lass, and returned to his Patagonian home.

Donald MacKay was born on 2 October 1928 in Patagonia. His father and mother had both been Caithness people; his father, James Murray MacKay, had been born at Geislittle near Thurso on 11 July 1903, the son of Benjamin MacKay, a farmer, and Mary (née Coghill). Donald's mother was Catherine Mowat, born on 31 December 1897 at Georgemas railway station in Caithness, where her father was a railway employee. Catherine's mother was Christina Malcolm.

James Murray MacKay married **Catherine Mowat**, a schoolteacher at Brawlbin in Caithness, on 3 September 1924. Then on 11 September James and Catherine departed for Buenos Aires. A family memory recalls that James, entranced by the tales of Caithness Patagonian Robert Nicolson on one of his visits to Caithness, had accepted his offer of employment at his Patagonian estancia; and another husband and wife departed from Caithness for South America.

The MacKay family are long-standing Caithness farmers. James's grandfather, also James MacKay, had farmed at Toftingall, near Watten, before relocating to the farm of Geislittle, and his son, Benjamin, to become James Murray MacKay's father, continued to farm at Geislittle. James Murray MacKay himself was recorded on his marriage certificate as a farmer at Geislittle. His farming experience must have been quickly recognised in Patagonia, as he was employed as foreman at Estancia Candon Pardo by 1927.

That same year, on 13 February 1927, a son, Benjamin Sutherland, was born to James and Catherine MacKay at Puerto San Julián. The following year a second son, Donald Alexander , was also born at Puerto San Julián, on 2 October 1928.

A number of trips to and from Patagonia and Caithness followed. James, Catherine, Benjamin and Donald arrived at Plymouth from Buenos Aires on 10 May 1933, prior to travelling north to Geislittle. James returned to Patagonia alone on 28 October 1933, while the rest of the family remained until 20 January 1934.

On 3 June 1951 the family returned again, arriving in London *en route* to Thurso – but the significant trip in the MacKay history was in 1955. On 6 January 1955 Donald MacKay married Charlotte Wigmore MacLean in Thurso.

Charlotte MacLean was born to John MacLean and Isabella (née Sinclair) on 2 June 1932 at Barrogill Castle, Mey, in the north of Caithness. Barrogill Castle (now Castle of Mey) had also been the location of Charlotte's parents' marriage on 26 December 1930. Isabella's father, Lachlan Sinclair, had been employed as a gardener at the castle.

Donald and Charlotte MacKay, the newly married couple, departed for Patagonia on 5 February 1955. Later that year, with the birth of Santiago on 11 December 1955, another generation of Caithness Patagonians was born. Then on 14 April 1957 a daughter, Isobel MacKay, was born. This latest generation of the MacKay family visited Thurso for the first time in 1959. James Murray MacKay, by this time a widower, made a lone pilgrimage back to Thurso in June 1960.

Long-lost Relatives

Caithness and Patagonia will always be a long way away geographically from each other. In the late 19th and early 20th centuries the distance impacted much more on communications than it does today; the time between sending a letter and receiving a reply could be up to a year. In that space of time people changed addresses and changed their circumstances, which resulted in contact being lost. This happened in the case of the Oman brothers from Caithness; letters were exchanged for a period, but with the passing of the generations regular contact was lost. Today's improved communication methods have, however, rekindled the family's links.

Nicol and John Oman grew up on Caithness farms and both made a career in Patagonian farming. Nicol was born on 8 November 1881 at Lythmore in Caithness, and John was born at Aultnabreac on 1 October 1883. Their father was William Oman and their mother was Jamesina (née Swanson).

The name Nicolas runs through the generations; William Oman's father was Nicolas and William had a brother Nicolas as well. The name continues into the current generation.

In 1861, William's father Nicolas had been a ploughman at Houstry, Dunn, near Watten – where, incidentally, fellow Caithness Patagonian Pioneer William Begg lived. In 1871, while the Oman family continued to reside at Houstry, William by this time had found employment as a farm servant at the nearby farm of Scorrieclate. William and Jamesina Swanson married at Janetstown near Thurso on 4 June 1880; Jamesina had been born on 8 June 1861 at the farm of Oust near Westfield.

Nicol and John were the only sons in William's family, but four sisters followed – Eliza born 1886, Bella born 1888, Georgina born 1893, and Christina born 1897. The 1891 census records the family at Achoy, Watten, where William was employed as a shepherd and Nicol and John were scholars, probably at Lannergill School. By 1901 the family had moved to Drakrass, near Halkirk. William continued in employment as a shepherd while Nicol and John had 'flown the nest'; 19-year-old Nicol was employed as a shepherd at Skinnet farm near Halkirk, and John, 17, had secured the position of under-shepherd at Tister, near Bower.

Nicol is recorded as departing for Patagonia in August 1907. There is no extant record of John's departure, but the family memory is that the two brothers left together, with their dogs. John settled in Patagonia, at Rio Chico.

Nicol made a return journey to Scotland in June 1908 to marry Lily Brunton from Inverness. At the time of his marriage, on 27 June 1908, Nicol recorded his employment as a shepherd at Rio Lobos, Patagonia.

Lily (sometimes known as Dolly) was the daughter of a soldier, William Brunton. Her mother was Mary Ann (née MacKenzie). Lily had been born in Inverness on 3 October 1883, into a family of numerous brothers and sisters. Prior to her marriage, she had worked in the Caledonian Hotel in Inverness, and her marriage certificate recorded her address as 9 Market Brae, Inverness. Nicol and Lily departed for Patagonia shortly after the wedding, sailing from Liverpool in July 1908. Fellow Caithnesian Angus Robert Bain from Mavesy sailed on the same ship.

Unless the current generation who have reconnected can discover more, little is known of the Oman brothers' lives in Patagonia. Nicol worked in 1914 at Estancia Stag River in the south-west region of Santa Cruz province, and his descendants continue to live in Argentina. John was employed at Estancia Cancha Rayada in 1915 and died in Rio Chico on 18 November 1949. The date of Nicol's death remains unknown, but his wife Lily's death is recorded as 9 February 1966.

From Hotel to Frigorifico

The early 1920s in Patagonia was a time of considerable strife. Worker-led strikes in the refrigeration plants and on the estancias resulted in much bloodshed and anguish for many. Sheep farmers like the Bain brothers were innocently caught up in the dispute; John Cormack had his farm ransacked and his family terrorised by the revolutionaries. Alexander Nicol, another Caithness Patagonian pioneer, found himself at the heart of a dispute that became known as the War of the Stone Throwers.

Alexander William Henderson Nicol was born 6 January 1880 in the Bridge Street Hotel, Wick. He was last in the line of a number of Nicol children. His father, James Nicol, was a hotelkeeper and his mother was Janet (Jessie) (née Baikie). James had been born 1 July 1829 in Reay, and Janet had been born 17 December 1834 in Barrock, Caithness. As a 16-year-old, she had worked as a servant at Bower Schoolhouse for the headmaster, William Adie, and his family. Janet and James had married on 6 December 1860 at the Church of Scotland Manse in Wick; James was living in Wellington Lane, Wick, and working as a coachman. In 1861 the first of their children, John, was born, on 19 January. Later that year at the time of the census, James, Janet and son John were resident in Anderson's Lane, Wick. James's parents, John and Jane, also lived with them. James was at the time employed as an ostler.

A daughter, Helen, was born to James and Jessie in 1863. Helen continued to live at home until she married Francis MacHugh in 1885; the ceremony was performed in her father's hotel, by then known as the Caledonian Hotel. Francis MacHugh worked as a telegraph engineer, and he and Helen lived and brought up a family in Wick before eventually moving to Edinburgh.

James and Jessie's second son, also named James, was born 4 November 1864 at Anderson's Lane, Wick. James junior began his working life as a shopkeeper before becoming a posting master by 1891. In 1891, too, the family moved to the new Nicol's Station Hotel in Wick; up until that point James Nicol senior had been the lessee of the Caledonian Hotel. The plans for the new hotel had been initiated in 1878. James junior died on 14 November 1895 at the Station Hotel.

The position of posting master ran in the family. The role was to ensure that the horses used by the mail coaches were ready and cared for. James Nicol senior had in his younger days been a coachman himself, and then held the position of ostler for the hotel in Bridge Street, Wick. Both George Nicol, born 25 January 1873, and

Alexander William Henderson Nicol were to hold the position of posting master in 1901.

A daughter and another son had preceded George Nicol's birth: Jane Manson had been born 4 February 1867 and David Leith Nicol on 16 October 1869. David lived only a short life; he died at Bridge Street, Wick, on 23 May 1882, aged only 13. Ten years earlier, in 1872, another son, Alexander Wares, died at only four months; his name was to be honoured and carried on by Caithness Patagonian Alexander William Henderson Nicol. Tragedy for his family of origin continued, however, with the death of another child; Jessie Baikie survived less than a year, and died at Bridge Street, Wick, on 12 December 1876.

James Nicol senior retired as a hotelkeeper, and died on 15 April 1898 at Moray Street, Wick. His widow, Janet, and the remaining members of the family subsequently moved to 61 Dempster Street, Wick, where Janet died on 21 February 1911.

Sometime between 1901 and 1910 Alexander gave up his job as a posting master and travelled to Patagonia. In 1910 he returned to Wick to marry Janet Nicolson. Recorded on his marriage certificate as a ranchman, he married Janet at 62 Henrietta Street, Wick, on 1 September 1910. The two departed for Patagonia later in the same month.

Janet Nicolson was born 25 August 1885 in High Street, Wick. She was the daughter of Peter Nicolson, carter, and Jane Bain. Peter had been born 16 November 1849 in Thurso, and Jane in Wick in 1852. Peter and Jane married on 2 February 1872. In keeping with the times, the Nicolson family was large in number.

Their first child, David, was born in 1872. Alexander was born in 1874. George Bain was born in 1878, followed by Christina in 1880. The Nicolson family at the time of the 1881 census lived in Stafford Place, Wick.

1881 saw the birth of Barbara, and then in 1884 Mary was born. Janet was next in line, in 1885, preceding Maggie in 1888, Peter in 1890, William in 1893 and finally Donald in 1899.

The Nicolson family resided in Henrietta Street, Wick, at census time in 1891 and 1901. This continued to be Janet's residence until her marriage to Alexander Nicol in 1910.

On 10 November 1911 a son to Alexander and Janet, James Peter, was born in Rio Gallegas. He was baptised by the Patagonian itinerating minister, the Rev. Neil Mac-Coll, on 4 March 1912, and in 1913 Janet and her son James returned to Wick, while Alexander continued to live and work in Patagonia. There is no evidence to suggest that Alexander ever returned to Caithness, nor that Janet returned to Patagonia.

By 1916 Alexander was working at one of Patagonia's largest refrigeration plants, Frigorífico Bories, near Puerto Natalles. He was employed as an administrator, probably in charge of the sorting of the animals as they arrived at the plant. As such he was in a position of some trust and experience.

In 1919 Frigorífico Bories was the scene of a workers' revolt that became known as the War of the Stone Throwers; the workers at the plant took exception to their perceived low wages and poor conditions, and set about bombarding the owners and managers of the factory with stones. Among the ensuing melée, Alexander Nicol and two fellow workers managed to get away from the scene, but due to the continuing violence he was forced to hide among the hills for some days, around the nearby Estancia Dorotea.

Unfortunately not much more is known of Alexander's time in Patagonia. He continued to live and work somewhere in the vicinity of the Magellan region. At the inception of the Strait of Magellan Lodge in 1937, he is recorded as a member. His wife Janet (née Nicolson) lived on in Wick until her death on 19 April 1960. Their son, James Peter, became a barber and married in 1946.

The Wandering Shepherds [1]

Shepherding skills were an obvious requirement in Patagonia, so it is no great surprise to find Angus and Hugh McPherson heading from Caithness to Patagonia; their father, nicknamed 'the wandering shepherd', had had a long career of shepherding across various parts of Scotland before settling in Halsary in Caithness, so as children Angus and Hugh had become accustomed to moving. The McPherson shepherding gene goes back at least two further generations and fits the pattern of shepherds following the migration north of sheep farming. Angus and Hugh were the fifth generation of McPherson shepherds. Their oldest known ancestor, Hugh, probably born around 1750, was father to John, born in Durness c. 1773. His son Neil was born in Farr around 1800, and his son William was father to the Caithness Patagonian Pioneers Angus and Hugh.

Angus in particular seems to have inherited this wandering gene. Having left Caithness for Patagonia, he then moved to Canada, before once more returning to Patagonia. His brother Hugh also departed for Patagonia, returned to Caithness for a wife, then went back again to Patagonia before ultimately settling in Scotland.

William, the father of Angus and Hugh, has been born in Assynt, Sutherland, on 25 March 1824; his own father, Neil McPherson, had also worked as a shepherd. Meanwhile Anne (née Kerr), mother of Angus and Hugh, was also a native of Assynt. Her father, Hugh Kerr, followed that other common West Highland employment route of fisherman.

By 1861 William McPherson was employed as a shepherd at Glenbeg, Contin, Ross & Cromarty. Three children, Davina, Robert and Murdoch, made up the family at that time. A further son, Neil, and a daughter, Colina, preceded the birth of **Hugh McPherson** on 8 July 1866. By the time of the 1871 census the family had moved again, this time to Dyke in Morayshire, where a daughter, Ann, was born in 1869. A further son, William, born 1873, preceded the birth of Angus. The girls largely went into service as nursemaid, cook and kitchen maid. Of the boys, Robert and Murdoch joined Highland regiments; Ann married James Munro from Westerdale, and their son, John, was to follow Angus and Hugh to Patagonia.

Angus McPherson entered the world on 27 May 1875 in the parish of Auldearn, Nairnshire. The family was completed with the birth of Mary MacLeod in 1877, while the family lived near Tain. Mary became a teacher and taught at Lannergill School in Caithness, although she died aged just 19 of tuberculosis. In the 1881 census Hugh is listed as a 14 year-old shepherd at Hill of Nigg Farm, while Angus, aged six, was resident with the family at Stoneyfield, Rosskeen.

Hugh then joined the Caithness exodus to Patagonia. Along with fellow Caithness Patagonian Pioneer James Earsman, Hugh sailed from Liverpool to Punta Arenas in 1890. At the time of Hugh's departure Angus was, along with his father, mother and sister Mary, resident in Caithness, at Halsary. Angus and his sister Mary attended Spittal School, Angus having transferred there from Portmahomack School in 1885. Along with a number of other older pupils, he temporarily left school in May 1888 to work as a herd. He did however return to school in November 1888 to pass his Standard 3 exams.

Hugh made his first trip home from Patagonia in May 1896, and obviously enthused his brother Angus to also head to Patagonia; Angus sailed from Liverpool to Punta Arenas on 2 August 1897. By 1899 Angus was at Estancia San Gregorio, one of the largest Braun/Menendez estancias in the region.

Life in Patagonia at that time was tough for new arrivals. Angus McPherson was a diarist, and thanks to his writing a clear picture has been recorded of the early Patagonian shepherding life.

Over the years he filled some nine volumes of notes and drawings. The diaries are also peppered with quotes, especially by Robert Burns. The early entries leave us in little doubt as to the hardship the shepherds endured. Up to about 1906 both Hugh and Angus continued to be employed by La Sociedad Explotadora de Tierra del Fuego, the largest sheep-ranching enterprise in southern Patagonia.

Angus in one of his diary entries wished himself elsewhere on 4 July 1903:

Today is a great day in North America and I would like to be in New York today. How strange is human nature? Today I am sick of this country or at least the weary lonesome life, which we lead here, the same dreary job over and over again without even a woman's smile to help us along day after day. If I could sell my animals I would clear out right away to South Africa or Canada. I will never bring myself to like this part of the world. Let me live in a country where there is some life. It's as well to be in a prison as here. Tomorrow I may feel quite different, I think there is a storm gathering.

Angus did not, however, lie down to his despair. He seems to have acquired some shares in sheep and possibly horses. With the income from these and what he had saved, in 1906 he set about making his dream come true; he left Patagonia, and arrived in Liverpool on 10 July 1906. From there he made his way to Cochrane, near Calgary in Canada, where he purchased the Merino Cattle Ranch. The Canadian Pacific Railroad passed through Cochrane, offering an effective and economic method of sending stock to markets.

Hugh was also on the move in 1906. On 4 June he departed Punta Arenas and headed for Scotland. He too was a man with a purpose. On 26 September 1906 he married Caithness lass **Catherine MacKay**. She had been born in Smerral, Latheron, on 8 September 1885, daughter of farmer Robert MacKay and Jessie (née Cormack). The 1891 census lists Catherine among a numerous MacKay family resident at Lower Smerral.

In 1901 Catherine MacKay was living at the family home, and was employed as a domestic servant. Shortly after her marriage to Hugh, the two set sail for Patagonia. It appears that their time in Patagonia on this occasion was brief. Reputedly, Catherine did not like the life and certainly their first daughter, Mary, was born back in Scotland, at Westcott, Beauly, on 25 October 1907. By 1911, Hugh and family were temporarily resident in Halkirk at the home of his mother, Ann.

Angus McPherson took the matrimonial route in 1909. On 10 February 1909 he married Mary Marr Mellis Ritchie at Cochrane, Alberta, Canada. Mary was the daughter of Edinburgh-born Dr Thomas George Gordon Ritchie.

In Canada, Angus had originally farmed cattle, then in 1910 he sold the cattle herd and moved into horse rearing. A keen horseman, he at one time captained the Cochrane Polo Club. His family remember him as a horse enthusiast, even setting up a family polo team on his Patagonian farm. In 1912, Angus sold the Merino Ranch in Canada and returned to Patagonia, where he bought Estancia San Mauricio and promptly changed its name to Estancia La Margarita, in honour of his daughter Marguerite.

Angus was also to use some of his money to build a house for his mother in Halkirk. Esperanza House was built by 1913 and today continues to stand proudly, and although ownership has changed there remain pictures of the McPhersons on display. Angus and Mary made a trip to Halkirk in 1916, when his mother died. While they were in Halkirk, his son, William Robert, was born, on 29 January 1917.

On his return to Patagonia, Angus became something of a benefactor. To the town of Perito Merino he gifted sufficient land for a school to be built. Today his generosity is honoured and his legacy remembered by a housing complex being named after him.

Angus died in Buenos Aires on 16 June 1956. His ashes were scattered on his farm at Perito Merino.

Hugh took up farming in Scotland, firstly in Perthshire and then in Broxburn. He died on 28 December 1949 in Edinburgh. His wife Catherine also died in Edinburgh, on 27 March 1965.

---

1 Additional information kindly supplied by descendants William Wilson and Diana McPherson.

Never Long in One Place

Shepherding and farm work involved regular movement between farms. At each term time, farmers would seek to employ new workers. Some of the workers, unhappy with their place of employment, would seek new employers. In Scotland the feeing market[1] was the place where new work agreements were settled. In Patagonia too, shepherds and sheep farmers would naturally seek the best employment deals. William Begg seemed to have carried the tradition with him from Caithness to Patagonia. He can be traced at a number of different Patagonian sheep farms.

William Begg was born 23 May 1858 at Houstry, Dunn, near Watten. He was the son of William Begg and Ann Gunn, but his mother died in childbirth the following year, on 25 July 1859, whilst giving birth to his sister, Margaret. His older siblings were Catherine born c. 1854, Ann born c. 1856, and Peterina born 9 June 1857.

William Begg senior remarried on 22 February 1861 at the Free Church in Watten. His second wife was Johan MacKay, who had been born in Tongue Parish c. 1827. At the time of her marriage to William she worked as a house servant at Houstry. William was a farmer in his own right; in 1861 he farmed 46 acres at Houstry. His second marriage produced a number of half-brothers and half-sisters for William junior: James born 5 May 1861, Robert born c. 1863, Johan born c. 1864, Andrew born 26 March 1865, and John born c. 1867.

In 1871 William junior began his movement between farms. First he farmed with his uncle William C. Gunn at Backless, near Watten. Then in 1881 he was employed as a farm servant at West Watten Mains. Finally, on 28 August 1891, he sailed from Liverpool to Punta Arenas.

John Hamilton, originally from Wick, had already established himself as a sheep farmer in Patagonia and in 1891 he placed an advertisement in the *John O'Groat Journal* offering Caithness men work as shepherds in Patagonia. William Begg, along with fellow Caithness men John McKinnon and the brothers David and Donald Christian, were probably the first to respond to John Hamilton's recruitment drive.

As a Patagonian shepherd, William sampled life in a number of Patagonian locations: 1896 Otway; 1900 Lucachao, Monte Dinero; 1905 Springhill, Tierra del Fuego; 1906, Porvenir, Tierra del Fuego; and 1915, Estancia Sara. On 3 March 1896 he married Martha Harriet Munday, daughter of Joseph Munday, a gardener. The Munday family had sailed to Punta Arenas in 1894. Martha had been born in Ewelme, Oxfordshire, on 15 August 1874, and the 1895 Argentine census lists Martha working as a servant in Rio Gallegos. The Mundays were a well-known family in the village of Ewelme, and a local legend suggests that one branch of the family were subjected to a witch's curse!

The first child of William and Martha's marriage was William Ernest, born on 18 August 1896 at Otway. Next came Albert John, born 31 August 1897. A third son, Ernest Robert, was born on 8 March 1899, probably in Punta Arenas; William Ernest and Ernest Robert were to follow their father to become Patagonian shepherds. On 11 June 1901 Martha, now called Harriet, returned to Britain with the four oldest children, William Ernest, Albert John Grant MacKennon, Ernest Robert and Violet (Violet is not listed anywhere else). They sailed on the *Oravia* from Punta Arenas to Liverpool.

Later additions to the family were Daisy born 1903, Mabel born 1904, Annie born 1905 and George Edward Joseph born 1906. A further child, Gladys born c. 1913, sailed with her mother Harriet on board the *Victoria* from Punta Arenas, and arrived at Liverpool on 18 April 1916. The forwarding address was Harriet's original family home at Ewelme. On 9 October 1924 Martha Begg and a child, David aged eight, were recorded as travelling between Liverpool and Punta Arenas.

The departure address was Wyke Green, Osterley Park in Illingworth. Daughter Gladys returned to Punta Arenas on 8 January 1925, travelling with a family named Blackwood from Glasgow; at least some of the Begg children attended school in England, so these journeys were probably trips to or from school. Many of the children's names are replicated among other branches of the Munday family.

William is believed to have met his death in 1942, having been thrown from a horse. Martha (Harriet) died on 26 July 1973 and is buried in Rio Grande.

Members of the original Caithness Begg family are buried in the historic Caithness graveyard known as the Tomb of Dunn.

---

1 A gathering of people hoping to be employed as domestic servants or farm workers.

A Patagonian Nephew

Once the first of the Caithness men and women had begun to leave for and settle in Patagonia, we find a number of relatives following. The Bain family from Mavesy were prominent, with seven brothers and sisters settling in Patagonia, and a number of their relatives and neighbours also joined the exodus from Caithness. Hugh and Angus McPherson were to provide the impetus for their nephew, John Munro, to make South America his home.

John Munro was born at Backlass, Westerdale, on 13 May 1898. His father was James Munro, a farmer, and his mother was Annie (née Fraser McPherson), daughter of William McPherson, and sister of Caithness Patagonian Pioneers Hugh and Angus McPherson. At the time of her marriage, Annie was employed at Ackergill Tower. John Munro's grandfather, John Munro senior, had been a Caithness farmer of some significance, and tenant at Achlibster.

John Munro was the eldest of a relatively large family. Around 1905 the family resided at Houstry Mains, Halkirk. The 1911 census records the family at Houstry Mains: 'James Munro (farmer), Annie F. Munro, John Munro aged 12, William Munro aged 11, Thomas Munro aged 9, Mary Munro aged 7, Margaret Munro aged 5, Annie Munro aged 4, Elizabeth Munro aged 1'.

Following in the footsteps of his uncles, Hugh and Angus McPherson, John Munro sailed from Liverpool to Punta Arenas on 21 October 1920 and gained employment with Angus at Perito Moreno. During June 1927 he returned to the family home at Houstry, allegedly looking for a wife. He was obviously unsuccessful, as he sailed back alone to Patagonia in October 1927. He was not entirely alone on the trip: Donaldina Sinclair, sister-in-law of William Bain from Lybster, sailed on the same ship. Two years later, however, John did marry; on 27 March 1929 he was wed to Augusta Elena Christina Nilsson.

For health reasons, John and his family moved to Chile. As it transpired this was not the best decision; the Munro family was caught up in a significant volcanic eruption and earthquake that destroyed everything. John and his family re-established themselves, in Tolten in Chile, where he was instrumental in building the town. Luck was not on their side however, as Tolten was then the victim of a tsunami. John is particularly remembered for the work he did in planning and funding a new cemetery in the town. Ironically, on his death in 1961 he was one of the first to be interred in it. Descendants and relatives of John Munro continue to be in contact with one another.

More Caithness Brothers, and a Nephew

The area around Clyth and Lybster in Caithness provided Patagonia with a number of shepherds. Times were hard on the crofts, and considerable pressure was put on the tenants as the estate landlords sought to increase rents. The brothers Robert and Donald Nicolson from Clyth may have hoped to ease the burden on their parents by emigrating to Santa Cruz province, Patagonia.

Robert MacGregor Nicolson was born 19 October 1883 at the family home in Clyth. His father was John Nicolson, a crofter and fisherman, and his mother was Margaret (née MacGregor). John Nicolson was regarded as one of the foremost skippers in the area and he owned a boat called the Cornucopia. The 1881 census shows the family living at Newlands, Clyth.

Robert's brother, **Donald Nicolson**, was born two years later, on 28 November 1885, also at Clyth. But whereas Donald appears to have left for Patagonia by the time of the 1901 census, Robert continued to live at home, and at the age of 15 was working as a plasterer's apprentice. Then by 1905 he had made his way to Patagonia, and was initially employed by William Bain at Estancia Josefina. Come 1910, Robert had established his own farm, aptly named Estancia Nicolson, although it was also known as Estancia Don Roberto.

Robert was a regular traveller between Patagonia and Caithness. He returned to Lybster for the Patagonian winter months and usually took up residence in the Portland Arms Hotel, Lybster, where he kept a car; Robert Nicolson and his 'jaunting' car became a well-known sight around Lybster.

His first trip to Caithness seems to have been in 1911, after arriving at Southampton on 3 October. Donald Bain, who was also heading for Caithness on a matrimonial mission, accompanied Robert on this trip. In 1925 Robert listed his destination address as the North British Hotel in Edinburgh. In 1928 he again sailed from Patagonia, this time with William Bain, and acted as witness at the marriage in Wick of David Bain and Jessie Cormack before returning to Patagonia on 8 November 1928.

Robert's last recorded trip was in 1937, when he departed Southampton for Buenos Aires; at that time his address was given as Duncan's Temperance Hotel, Union Street in Glasgow.

Despite having the resources to make these trips across the Atlantic, life was not always easy for Robert Nicolson. A 1912 letter sent to his brother in Caithness states that on Estancia Nicolson shearing was 20,000 kilos down on the previous year. Eventually Robert passed on the ownership of his Patagonian farm to his nephew, Alexander Nicolson.

Alexander had been born at Mid Clyth, Caithness on 20 July 1917. His father was James Nicolson (Robert and Donald's brother). Alexander's mother was Williamina (née Smith Macleod), originally from Scarfskerry in Caithness. Alexander returned to visit family at Overtown, Clyth, in Caithness in 1955, when he brought with him his wife Rebecca (a Bain descendant), son Robert and daughter Margaret.

The Nicolson and Bain families were near neighbours in Caithness, and in Patagonia the association continued, with the marriage of Alexander Nicolson and Lola Rebecca MacDonald on 26 April 1947. Lola was the daughter of Rebecca (née Bain) and her husband, Lachlan MacDonald.

Alexander's father, James, died on 22 January 1962 and Alexander's mother, Williamina, on 29 November 1979. They are buried in Clyth cemetery, and their headstone also commemorates Alexander, who died in Patagonia on 14 October 1986 and is interred in Comodora Rividavia.

Details of Donald Nicolson are a little sketchy. In 1914 he is listed among those who donated to the *Magellan Times* Widows and Orphans Fund. His address at the time was Estancia Esperanza.

Left: Estancia Morro Chico – still part of the John Hamilton family business

Below: Once one of the largest sheep farms in Patagonia

Left and below: Frigorifico Bories railway system

Clockwise from left:

A Caithness Patagonian set of bagpipes

James Plowman - dressed for Patagonia

Log House built by Hugh and Angus McPherson

*Shipping lists track the movement
of the Caithness Patagonians*

Sheep shearing - a skilled job

John Hamilton Street in Rio Gallegas

Left: Asado - the Patagonian Barbeque

Right: Luggage for a seven week sea crossing

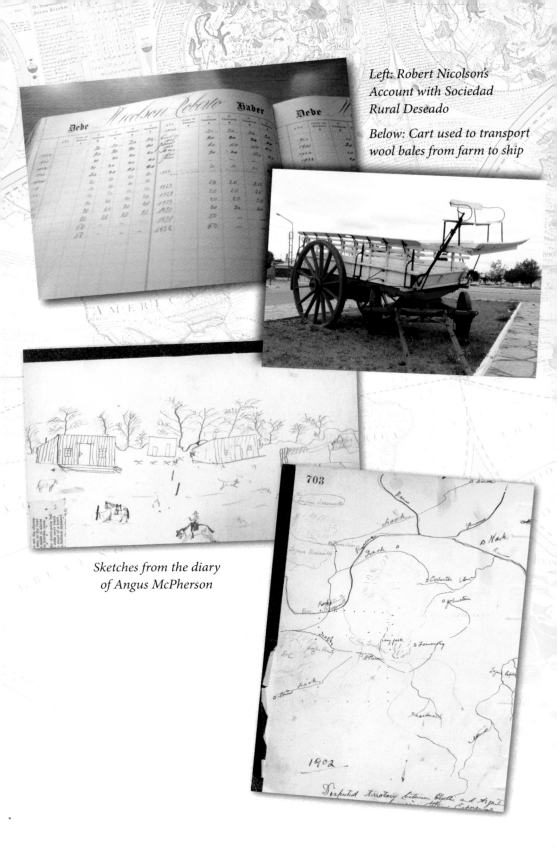

Left: Robert Nicolson's Account with Sociedad Rural Deseado

Below: Cart used to transport wool bales from farm to ship

Sketches from the diary of Angus McPherson

Sociedad Rural Deseado lists the Bain brothers from Mavesy among its founders

Patagonian sheep

Patagonia - a vast bleak landscape

A Patagonian Gaucho

*The school in Fitzroy
– now twinned with
Lybster Primary*

Above: Sheep medicine from Scotland

Left: One of Hamilton & Saunders many estancias

Sheep, sheep and more sheep…

Three Brothers Go to Argentina

During the infamous Highland Clearances, when sheep were replacing people across the north of Scotland, there was a demand for experienced shepherds. Into the northern region from the Borders came a number of shepherds who had developed skills and expertise in managing large flocks of sheep. One of them was John Earsman. Three of his sons were to make lives for themselves in Argentina, two recruited for the growing sheep farming industry in Patagonia. The third went to work on the equally expanding Argentine railway.

John Earsman had been born in Wamphrey, Dumfries, on 3 August 1832, son of John Earsman, shepherd, and Jane Irvine. Young John's first wife, Margaret (née Murray), had been born in 1838 at Crawford, Lanarkshire.

By 1865 John and Margaret Earsman had moved north, and a son, **William Earsman**, was born on 27 June at Golval, Strath Halladale. The 1871 census records the family at Borgie, near Tongue, where John was employed as a shepherd. A second son, **James Earsman**, was born on 19 May 1870 at Borgie. Both William and James later departed for South America.

Another son, **George Earsman**, was born in 1873 at Borgie, and he too was to set off for extreme parts of the world; he became a prospector in the Yukon, and died in Vancouver in 1942.

Tragedy struck the family on 12 September 1875 when Margaret died. No cause of death is given on the death certificate, but a notice of her death was printed in the *John O'Groat Journal*:

> At Borgie on the 12th September, Maggie, the beloved wife of Mr John Earsman, sheep manager, Borgie, Sutherlandshire. Friends at a distance will please accept this intimation.[1]

John Earsman married again, on 8 February 1877. His second wife was Isabella Piercy, daughter of John Piercy, salmon fisher on the Naver (so by this time, the Piercy family had moved from Northumberland up to Sutherland), although Isabella had been born in Northumberland, around 1850. The Earsman family continued to grow in number and prosper.

By the 1881 census, John Earsman was sheep manager at Hallum House, Reay. In 1884 the family moved again, to Todholes in Lyth and it was here that **Percy**

Earsman, to become the third of the Earsman Argentine pioneers, was born on 21 April 1888.

At the time, the Todholes area of Lyth was a collection of crofts, none of which remain. Todholes was situated just off the old Lyth–Hastigrow drove road; in this area there existed a compound where the animals and drovers would rest on their long journey south – an interesting parallel with the sheep drover routes in Patagonia.[2]

While resident at Lyth, John Earsman became an active member of Bower Church. He was appointed to the Committee for Church Defence on 27 July 1895, and in July 1904 he was appointed an elder of Bower Parish Church. Interestingly, at Todholes the Earsman family were neighbours of the MacKay family – and Helen and Jane MacKay also went to Patagonia, as the wives of George and Angus Bain respectively.

James Earsman departed for Patagonia on 28 October 1890, along with fellow Caithness shepherd Hugh McPherson.

Although there is no exact date as to when William set sail, there was a William Earsman listed in Buenos Aires in the 1895 Argentine census. By 1897 he was resident in Bahia Blanca, where he married Emily Jane Isabella Saunders.

James was by this time resident in Patagonia, and around 1904 he married Hannah MacCall Cameron, who was also a descendent of a Scottish family in Patagonia. James had initially been employed as a shepherd by the huge Patagonian sheep farming company Explotadora; by 1906 he had become manager at Estancia Stag River.

James went on to purchase a Patagonian farm near Puerto Natales where he established a slaughterhouse and butcher shop that served the local village. He was obviously a community person; to help bring the community together he established a social club in Puerto Natales.

John Earsman died in Lyth on 20 April 1910, leaving behind his wife Isabella, son Percy and daughter Lizzie at home in Lyth. Percy then joined his half-brothers in Argentina in August 1912, sailing from Liverpool to Buenos Aires on 22 August.

James Earsman brought his wife, Hannah Mary, and one-year-old son James to Scotland in June 1914. Hannah Mary and son James returned to Britain again in 1916; the passenger list gives an address in South Wales. James junior then spent his formative years in Scotland. In 1924 he returned to Patagonia, having spent 12 years at school in Scotland.

Some form of family gathering must have taken place in 1923. William Earsman, with his wife Emily and daughter Jeanie, arrived in Britain in April 1923. On the passenger lists, he was described as a railway official and later as a railway inspector. James and Percy Earsman also arrived from Patagonia in 1923; Percy's destination address was 1 McLeay Street, Wick.

Percy began to travel the world. In May 1927 he set sail from Patagonia for Liverpool, then in July 1927 he sailed from London to Adelaide in Australia. Around the same time, James's wife Hannah began to make a series of trips from Patagonia to Britain. In September 1928 her destination address was James Place, Brought Ferry. On a number of other occasions between 1930 and 1935 she provided addresses in Manchester and Carnoustie.

Percy's mother Isabella died on 5 April 1932, and is buried alongside her husband in Bower Cemetery.

James died on 13 April 1936 at Hospital Calle Bories, 451, Magallanes, Chile; he is buried in Punta Arenas Cemetery.

Percy married Margaret Matilde Craik Sutherland, daughter of Alexander Sutherland, originally from Brora. The date of their marriage is unclear, but Percy, along with Margaret, visited his sister's home in Dunnett Avenue, Wick, in 1952. It is possible they remained in Scotland until 15 January 1954, when Percy and Margaret were listed as outgoing passengers from Southampton to Buenos Aires. The address provided on this occasion was 31 St Claire Crescent, Roslin, which had a connection with the Sutherland family.

Percy Earsman died on 7 July 1965, and is buried in Rio Gallegas, Patagonia.

---

1 *John O'Groat Journal* 16/9/1875.
2 Thanks to Stephen Pottinger, Barrock Mains.

The Christian Brothers

The Caithness Patagonian story is littered with examples of emigrating brothers. The Bain brothers were the most significant in terms of number, but add to that the Nicolson brothers, the McPherson brothers, the Sutherland brothers, the Mackenzie brothers, the Hendry brothers, the Earsman brothers, the Plowman brothers, the Harper brothers and the Oman brothers. The three Christian brothers complete the list.

Donald and David Christian were the first to go to Patagonia, in 1891 while Henry, the youngest of the three, departed in 1897. They all travelled with other Caithness Patagonian emigrants.

Donald was the eldest of the family. Born on 1 May 1856 at Bowermadden, he was followed by a number of brothers and sisters. His parents were David Christian and Jane (née Horne). David had been born in Wick in 1835, while Jane was one year older, born in Canisbay Parish in 1834; David and Jane had married on 15 December 1854 at Bower. After Donald came two more sons – James in 1858 and John in 1860 – and at the time of the 1861 census the family were still resident at Bowermadden.

David was born 30 August 1863 at Bowermadden. Then in 1867 a daughter, Esther Christian, was born. The following year Henry was born, on 11 May 1868, but by this time the family had moved to Stirkoke. The birth of Margaret in 1870 completed the family. The 1871 census lists David Christian senior as a farmer of 14 acres, but in June of that year he died following a relatively short illness.

Donald at first enlisted in the army. In 1881 he was stationed at Fort George. Ten years later he was one of the first men from Caithness to join the Patagonian trail; he joined his brother David, William Begg and John MacKinnon in a group that appears to have been the first to respond to John Hamilton's recruitment advertisement. They sailed from Liverpool for Punta Arenas on 28 August 1891, on the *James Watt*.

Younger brother Henry had learned the trade of tailoring. In 1881 he lived with the rest of the Christian family at Newton near Wick, and it may be worth speculating that he worked with the Hamilton firm of clothiers in Wick. John Hamilton's younger brother James was running the business by this time, and given that Henry's two brothers were among the first to respond to the Hamilton Patagonian recruitment drive, a Hamilton association with the Christians seems possible.

Henry, however, left the tailoring trade behind and sailed from Liverpool to Punta Arenas on 7 October 1897, on board the *Oravia*; his brother David must have returned to Wick by this time, as he too is listed as a passenger on the *Oravia*. Two others from Caithness also joined this ship *en route* to Patagonia: David Barnetson and Andrew Harper made up the contingent.

Donald returned home in 1900, arriving on 29 April, and returned to Patagonia again on 18 October 1900. By 1901 the Christian household was residing at Old Stirkoke, where Jane, now in her seventies, lived with her son James and his family. David returned again to Britain in 1903, this time with his wife and two children, John and Esther. David departed again, alone, on 15 October 1903, but was back again in Caithness in June 1904. This time he departed for Patagonia, along with his wife, in October 1904 – but there is no record of the children returning: did they remain in Britain?

Henry was next to return to Caithness for a short period. He arrived on 8 May 1905 and departed again on 14 September 1905. Two more Caithness men joined him – John Mowat and Sinclair Bremner.

Tragedy struck the family however, as Donald died on board the *Oropessa*, having been taken ill while travelling between Punta Arenas and Liverpool in September 1906.

Henry was also in Britain in 1906. He departed from Southampton for Buenos Aires on 14 December 1906 with his new wife; he had married Alexandrina Dunnet from Wick, and so she joined that unique group of Caithness Patagonian women.

In 1912 David Christian also arrived in Britain with his wife and family. His employment status was recorded as an ironworker, and along with Elizabeth, aged 40, Esther Maud (10), Daisy Ladouch (6) and Margaret (5), he arrived in Liverpool on 8 July 1912.

By 1925 Henry was a farm manager in Patagonia, and he began to make plans for his eventual return to Caithness. He returned to Wick on 28 April 1925 along with Alexandrina, giving a forwarding address of Dunvegan House, Wick. The couple departed again on 7 August 1926, but in 1928 they left Patagonia for the final time and returned to Wick, where they lived initially at 7 Harbour Terrace before making a later move to 6 Sinclair Terrace. Alexandrina died there on 12 December 1950, and Henry passed away on 13 September 1958.

An Argentinian Family

The majority of the men who left Caithness for Patagonia either returned to Caithness to marry, or married wives from within the British Argentine community. David Barnetson, however, chose a different route; his bride, Anna Cozzetti, was an Argentinian.

David Barnetson was born on 3 October 1876 in Kirk, Caithness. Though he was initially registered as illegitimate, his father and mother subsequently married and went on to have a further six children. David's father, David Barnetson senior, and his mother, Margaret (née Fairweather), had married on 15 June 1877 at Kirk. Margaret's father, David Fairweather, was a farmer of 21 acres at Kirk in Caithness.

David Barnetson was born into a farming family and as such often moved home. In 1881 the Barnetson family lived at Hempriggs, near Wick, and in 1891 at Newton, Wick. David Barnetson senior was an agricultural labourer on these farms. The family grew in number when William was born on 1 May 1878. Peter was born 28 May 1880 (only to die aged just 13, on 28 August 1893 at Hempriggs). On 14 September 1882 James was born at Hempriggs, as was Henrietta Bain on 23 September 1884. Two more children followed: Ephraim Fairweather was born on 23 October 1887, and finally Jane (Jeannie) Bella on 8 September 1890.

David left for Patagonia in 1897, departing from Liverpool to Punta Arenas on 7 October. Two other Caithness men sailed on the same boat: Henry Christian and Andrew Harper.

At the time of the 1901 census, the Barnetson family, now minus David, lived at Loch Side Farm, Hempriggs. By 1911 David Barnetson senior, his wife, son James and daughter Jeannie, lived at 10 Bridge Street in Wick.

In 1903 David applied for a lot of land near Puerto San Julián, within the government's 1882 low-price offer. According to Patagonian sources he was refused because at the time he had a broken leg. However, with the help of a reference from fellow Caithnesian Angus Bain, David gained employment in the local refrigeration plant.

Back home in Scotland, David's brother William married Isabella Hutchison in Edinburgh in 1905, and his sister Henrietta married Robert Pope, an Edinburgh policeman, on Christmas Day 1908. She worked as a mental nurse, and by the time of the 1911 census was resident at 2 Glenogle Place, Edinburgh.

Two years later David married Ana Cozzetti, on 26 March 1910. Ana was an Argentine citizen and had been born in 1893. David's family back in Caithness had urged him to visit them, and he did contemplate doing so – but by the time he was able to make any arrangements the First World War had broken out and it was considered too dangerous a journey. Unlike most of the Caithness Patagonians, David Barnetson never returned to Caithness.

David and Ana had a number of children, who contributed to public life in Patagonia. Santiago David Barnetson was born on 18 August 1911. He went on to own a hotel in Puerto Deseado. On 9 March 1914 a son, Epfrain, was born at San Julián. He became a key figure in the town of Puerto Deseado; he ran the town's newspaper, *El Orden*, and with his brother Eduardo played a leading role in the establishment and running of the local football team, Deseado Juniors. Eduardo had been born in c. 1915 in Puerto Deseado. Daughter Margarita was born in Puerto Deseado on 28 November 1915. Then in 1918 another son, Alberto, was born in Puerto Deseado, and in 1921 a second daughter, Teresa . She was to continue the family tradition of involvement with the Deseado Juniors; in 1936 she put her creative skills into embroidering handkerchiefs, displaying the colours and logo of the football team.

Both of David's parents died within a short period of each other. His mother Margaret died in 1921, and in 1923 David senior passed away. Both died in Edinburgh, at 29 Iona Street. Within another two years, David's sister Henrietta also died in Edinburgh.

Prior to this, another daughter of David and Ana, named Isabel, had been born, on 29 March 1923. The family was complete on 29 May 1925, with the birth of Alejandro.

Ana died in 1942. In recognition of his Argentinian wife and family, who spoke only Spanish, David applied for Argentine citizenship, and this was granted in 1947. David died on 20 May 1953 and is buried in Puerto Deseado, the town he made his home.

Patagonian Pipers

The piping tradition remains important amongst the current generation of Caithness Patagonians. The descendants of Rebecca Bain and Lachlan MacDonald continue the Tiree piping tradition, and many others of Scots origin were pipers across South America. The name most often associated with the bagpipes among the Caithness Patagonian Pioneers is that of Plowman; Alexander and George Plowman were pipers at many Patagonian gatherings.

George Plowman and his brother Alexander both made their way to Patagonia, following in the footsteps of their father, James Plowman. James's tales of Patagonia must have encouraged his two sons to emigrate. George eventually returned to Caithness, while Alexander made his home in Patagonia.

James Plowman was born 13 February 1868. His father was also James and his mother was Catherine (née MacDonald). James spent his early years at East Clyth, initially living with the family of Donald and Christina MacKay on their croft. By 1881 his address was Warehouse, Clyth, and in 1891 James is recorded as an East Clyth farmer living with his mother, Catherine, as housekeeper.

James left for Patagonia around 1892. Prior to his departure the Clyth Ploughing Association had presented him with an inscribed watch and chain. James, it seems, would have left for Patagonia with the intention of returning to marry his sweetheart, Sinclair Bain, the daughter of Alexander Bain and Sinclair Sinclair from Mavesy. But his intended, alas, died on 14 September 1897, before James reached Scotland to marry her.

On his return to Caithness on 26 August 1900, to mark her death and to help express his sorrow, James erected a memorial headstone in Clyth Cemetery that reads:

Erected by James Plowman, Straits of Magellan, in remembrance of his beloved betrothed Sinclair Bain, (born c. 1866) daughter of Alexander Bain, who died 14th September 1897, aged 31 years – 'many waters cannot quench love neither can the floods drown'.

On 24 January 1901 he married Sinclair's sister, Margaret Bain. Initially the couple resided with Margaret's parents at Mavesy, Lybster, but by the time of the birth of their daughter, Sinclair Bain, on 10 June 1901 they had moved to Mybster, in the centre of Caithness. A son, James, was born at Balbeg on 28 February 1903. A daughter, Annie, was also born at Balbeg on 18 November 1904. The first of the Plowman Patagonian brothers, **Alexander Plowman**, was born at Balbeg on 4 December 1908. The next son, Donald, was born 21 October 1909. On 2 October 1911 **George Plowman** was born at Balbeg, and in 1917 the final member of the family, Thomas Saunders, was born. (There can be little doubt that Thomas, the youngest in the family, was named in remembrance of James's days in Patagonia; there he had met the Thomas Saunders who had been the partner of Wick man John Hamilton and one of the first of the Patagonian sheep farmers.) Living with the family at Balbeg in 1911 was James Plowman's mother, Catherine. She died at the farm on 20 October 1922.

Alexander set sail for Patagonia on 21 September 1928. On the same ship were the brothers David and William Bain and their respective wives and families.

Alexander was a well-respected member of the Halkirk area community and a successful local athlete; he was twice winner of the Sir Archibald Sinclair Cup for athletics and a winner of the Halkirk Athletic Gold Medal. To mark his departure for Patagonia a memorial evening was held in Spittal, where he was presented with a gold watch and chain, plus a wallet of treasury notes.

By 1939 he was working at Estancia Leon in Patagonia. Today this estancia sits within the Monte Leon National Park and like many of the original Patagonian estancias is now available as tourist accommodation.

Alexander married Sarah Ann Walker on 7 June 1941 and continued to live in Patagonia. At the time of his death on 25 March 1964, he was an administrator at Estancia Stag River.

George Plowman followed his brother Alexander to Patagonia in 1929 sailing from London on board the *Highland Monarch*. There was quite a Caithness contingent aboard; in the company of George Plowman was William Budge plus George Bain and family. George visited his homeland in 1960, and again in 1984, before finally returning to Caithness in 1990. In June 1994, he died in Caithness.

Today in Patagonia, George Plowman is fondly remembered as a friend and a great piper.

A Band of Shearers

A number of Caithness Patagonian Pioneers were musical. Members of the Plowman family were and still are renowned pipers. Angus McPherson reputedly asked his mother to dispatch an accordion to Patagonia, and memories exist of his 'box' playing well into his later years. The name of Harper, too, is today synonymous with music in Caithness; Addie Harper and the Wick Scottish Dance Band were internationally known from the 1950s onwards, and the 21st-century Caithness musicians owe much of their success to the teaching and encouragement of the current generation's Addie Harper.

The Harper musical heritage can be traced back to his grandfather, Robert, affectionately known as Robbie 'sheep shearer' Harper. He reputedly collected many tunes from his fellow Patagonian shepherds, especially those who had originated in Lewis, in the Outer Hebrides. Robert's brother, Andrew, was also a very fine musician. Both Harper brothers were among the Caithness Patagonian Pioneers.

Andrew Harper was born in Sarclet, Caithness, on 30 June 1877. He was the second son of James Harper, a wool weaver, and Williamina (née Sutherland) who had come from Knockinnon, near Dunbeath. James had been born in Wick in 1853, the son of Andrew Harper and Catherine Christian. Williamina, who was three years older than her husband, had been born in 1850 in the Parish of Latheron, daughter of James Sutherland and Catherine (née Henderson). James and Williamina married at Achairn, Stirkoke, on 21 May 1875.

Andrew had an older brother, a second James, who was born in 1875 but who died on 28 April 1883 at the age of only 13. Another brother, John, was born in 1880. At the 1881 census the family resided at Stirkoke, where James Harper was established in his trade as a woollen weaver. Andrew was to depart for Patagonia on 7 October 1897, along with two other Caithness Patagonians – David Barnetson and Henry Christian. Andrew returned to Caithness in June 1906 and, along with his brother Robert, set off for Patagonia again on 27 September 1906.

Robert Harper was born on 28 April 1883 at West Banks in Wick, and another brother, James S., was born in 1890. The youngest in the family, George, was born in 1892.

By 1901 Robert was employed as a farm servant, on the farm of Donald Meiklejohn at Kilimster; meanwhile, James and the rest of the family were resident at

7 Oldwick Road, Wick in 1901, where James continued to work as a woollen weaver.

Robert returned home in 1914, arriving at Liverpool from Punta Arenas on 3 February. Andrew returned to Caithness from Patagonia later, in May 1922. The two brothers brought back to Caithness their musical skills plus their sheep-shearing skills; they are remembered in Caithness for their speed and dexterity at shearing. The ability to use both hands to shear was unusual and may have been helped by their equal dexterity at playing fiddle and accordion. Andrew's family also recall him displaying his lasso talents, picking off sheep at will with a rope.

Robert married Marjory Lockie on 7 June 1918. She was a dressmaker at the time of her marriage, while Robert was by then employed as a ploughman at the farm of Ackergill Mains. Marjory also came from sheep farming stock; her father, John Lockie, had been a shepherd on the farm of Lynegar. Her mother was Jessie (née Taylor).

Andrew Harper married Bella Gunn from Newton on 7 July 1922 and settled firstly in the Thrumster area and later in the Reay and Dounreay district.

A Patagonian Tragedy

The Halkirk area of Caithness produced a number of Patagonian emigrants. Among them were two MacKenzie brothers, Alexander and William. Alexander, who developed a serious medical condition, eventually returned to Caithness. William, however, lost his life in Patagonia.

Alexander MacKenzie was born at Forsie in Caithness on 29 July 1885. His father was also Alexander MacKenzie, a shepherd. His mother was Christina (née Elder), daughter of a landed proprietor in Caithness. Alexander, along with his father, mother, sisters and brothers, lived at Achater at the time of the 1891 census.

William MacKenzie was born 4 November 1894, also at Forsie. By 1901 the family, including both Alexander and William, are listed as resident at South Calder in Caithness.

Christina, mother of the MacKenzie brothers, died on 2 December 1938 at Achaguie, Scotscalder, and their father, Alexander, died on 21 February 1945. Thus the parents were at least spared the news of their son William's untimely death in Patagonia, on 22 April 1947.

The date of Alexander's departure for Patagonia is unclear, but there is an Alexander MacKenzie listed as a passenger returning to Britain in July 1908. William remained at South Calder at least until 1911. It is known that Alexander, who had settled in the San Julián area of Patagonia, was a guest at the British Club in Punta Arenas on 28 February 1912.

Alexander made another trip to the family home at Achaguie, Halkirk, during February 1925. This trip home seems to have sparked William's decision to follow his brother, for William departed London for Buenos Aires on 26 February 1925. Alexander returned again to Britain during October 1931. He is known to have developed throat cancer and was treated in a London hospital where his voice box was removed and an artificial device inserted in its place. Family reminiscences suggest that this operation may have taken place during a further return trip to Britain.

Some mystery still surrounds William's death in 1947. Legend has it that he was murdered, but a stone in Rio Gallegas Cemetery suggests that he died in the 'line of duty'. What this 'line of duty' was has not been established, but his burial was organised by the Sociedad Anon Imp. y Exp. de la Patagonia, one of the companies in the Braun Menendez empire. If they had been his employer, then he presumably died carrying out some employment duty. A memory of his relatives in Caithness points towards his intervention in some dispute which resulted in his death. Alexander was concerned at not being able to help, or indeed be present. This version suggests that it happened during the time that Alexander was in London for his throat operation, and it is to some extent borne out by the fact that the above company organised the burial.

The result of Alexander's throat operation left him with difficulty in speaking. Instead he used a pencil and notepad as his means of communication. Some of the current older generation in San Julián, Patagonia, fondly remember Alexander riding into town from his estancia, and checking into the local hotel before making his base in the San Julián British Club. From here he communicated via his pencil and notebook, which apparently was the source of some risqué stories and jokes. Unfortunately for today's historians, Alexander simply tore out the pages and discarded them.

Alexander returned to Caithness in his later years, firstly to the family home at Achaguie, then into a house in Halkirk. He died on 4 October 1971.

Tough Luck

The fortunes of those from Caithness who departed for Patagonia were varied. Some became successful sheep farmers; some returned to Caithness; and some felt the full rigours of the climate and frontier lifestyles of Patagonia. John Cormack's experiences in Patagonia can only be described as momentous – yet he bounced back from a number of setbacks to raise a Patagonian family.

John Cormack was born on 18 December 1870 at Achow, Lybster, in Caithness. His mother was Ann Cormack, but his father is not recorded. Ann lived at Achow with her parents, John and Ann Cormack, plus a brother, sisters, nieces and nephews.

John Cormack arrived in Rio Gallegas, Patagonia, around 1904 and worked at Punta Loyola for Hamilton & Saunders (John Hamilton's firm). Apart from working with sheep, John Cormack put his skills as a carpenter to good use, firstly at Punta Loyola, and then when he set up his own estancia at North Hills. Here he built a wooden house. Following the trend of returning to Scotland for a Caithness bride, on 8 September 1905, he married Annie Chapman at St Peter's Church, Gardener Street, in Glasgow.

Annie Chapman was also originally from the Lybster area of Caithness. She was born on 8 April 1883 at Upper Lybster, the daughter of William Chapman, a butler, and Jessie (née Bain). In 1901 the family residence was 56 Crossburn Street, Glasgow, at which point Jessie had become a widow while Annie worked as a dressmaker.

Annie, having married John Cormack in 1905, moved with him to Patagonia; her mother Jessie subsequently joined her daughter and son-in-law in Patagonia, where she lived and died.

Over the years John and Annie's family grew in number. First born was Janet, c. 1906, followed by Donald, Charles, George, Alexander, Annie Minnie, Ruth (Polly) and Daisy.

John's attempts at establishing himself in Patagonia were, however, ill-fated. First, while at North Hills he was forced to vacate his farm; it was claimed that the land belonged to Hamilton & Saunders, although his family always maintained that this was simply a ruse to move him on. John, never daunted, set up again at Mendi Aike, only to subsequently find himself and his family caught up in a 1920s workers' revolution. John was one of the innocent casualties of Patagonia's workers' revolt. During the 1920s a workers' strike escalated into a bloody dispute that disrupted many farms.

John descendants recalled their experience:

One day the strikers passed through Mendi Aike and they took some of the staff by force, except for one who managed to hide. Mummy would tell that they entered the storeroom and they ate the eggs raw. She had no choice but to let them take what they wanted and she asked them not to touch her children. They took the horses and only left the one for the guard. Mummy was expecting Polly and everyone advised that the families shouldn't stay at the estancias, so the Taylors at Barranca Blanca brought us to Gallegas and we stayed at the hotel Londres. Dad stayed at the estancia with that labourer and the schoolmaster.[1]

Family education was important to John and Annie; they employed a live-in teacher and built a schoolroom which was kitted out with

desks with inkwells made of lead; teacher's desk; the board and also a blackboard for each of us, they wrote a finite black pencil, which we erased with a sponge.[2]

However John was forced to set up yet another new home. Economically times were hard for Patagonia's smaller sheep farming businesses, and in an attempt to keep his business afloat he auctioned off his property in 1934 and moved for a third time. His daughter Daisy recalled how 'this situation of the auction and the move was so costly it affected Dad's health, and in a few years he died.'[3]

John died on 18 July 1936 and is buried in Rio Gallegas Cemetery. His wife Annie, several years younger than him, died in 1971.

---

1 Club Britannica Rio Gallegas.
2 Pablo Beecher interview notes.
3 Club Britannica Rio Gallegas.

Rest in Peace

Many of the original Caithness Patagonian Pioneers rest in peace in Patagonia. Cemeteries in towns such as Puerto Deseado, Puerto San Julián, Rio Gallegas and Punta Arenas commemorate their lives. Most lived relatively long, productive and peaceful lives, although one or two met with an untimely death.

Most painful, of course, is the death of a child, and it would seem that in the case of John and Williamina McKinnon the loss of three children in Patagonia was simply too much to cope with in a foreign land.

John Grant McKinnon had been born 14 September 1871 at Shielton near Watten. The farm of Shielton lies well into inland Caithness, and the wide open outlook that John had grown up with would have prepared him, to some extent, for the vast plains of Patagonia. John's parents were Donald McKinnon and Margaret (née Robertson). They had married on 25 June 1852, and brought up a number of sons and daughters prior to the birth of John, their youngest child. First born was James in 1853. Alex H. came next in 1854, followed by Isabella in 1856. 1858 saw the birth of Lachlan, then in 1860 Catherine, followed by Mary in 1861; in that year Donald was farming 142 acres at Shielton.

The family numbers had increased again in 1864 with the birth of Jane; then in 1865 William was born. Next in line was George, born in 1867 before the youngest, John, in 1871. By 1881 only John remained at Shielton with his father and mother, but by the age of 20 John had also left home, sailing in August 1891 for Patagonia.

John McKinnon was one of the earliest Caithness men to leave for Patagonia. Along with a near neighbour, William Begg, and the brothers Donald and David Christian from the Wick area, they are the first recorded recruits that responded to John Hamilton's 1891 advertisement seeking shepherds in Patagonia.

By 1905 John was employed within the Última Esperanza area of Chilean Patagonia. On 20 May 1907 he arrived in Liverpool from Punta Arenas with matrimony in mind, and on 14 November 1907 he married Williamina MacDonald Sutherland at the Watten United Free Church.

Williamina Sutherland was born on 13 February 1879 at her parents' farm near Wick. Her father was James Henderson Sutherland and her mother was Colina (née MacKay MacDonald). Williamina was the fifth of the Sutherland children, preceded by Hughina, Margaret, Jane and James.

Four more sisters and brothers were born to James and Colina over the following decade: Jessie was born 1883; Roderick born 1885; John born 1887; and William P. S. in 1889. Eight of the children were still in residence at the family farm near Milton, Wick, in 1891. At the 1901 census, Williamina, along with her parents and various brothers and sisters, lived at Newton near Watten, which was not too far from the McKinnon farm at Shielton.

A new life in Patagonia now awaited Williamina and John, and in 1910 a son, Donald Alexander, was born to them. Obviously keen to share the joy of their new addition, John and Williamina plus baby Donald visited Caithness, arriving at Liverpool on 19 April 1910. After their return to Patagonia, a daughter, Colina Margaret Jane, was born, in 1913. Then, in 1916 a second son, James, was born, to be followed in 1918 by the birth of Benjamin. The youngest of the sons, Gilbert George Edward, was born in Rio Gallegas on 7 December 1920. The youngest child of all, Mary Alice, was born in 1921.

Shortly after this, a triple tragedy struck the McKinnon family. Six-month-old Mary, eight-year-old Colina and eleven-year-old Donald all died in 1921. Their short lives are marked with a gravestone in Rio Gallegas Cemetery. This was probably too much for the MacKinnon family to bear, and on 15 October 1924 John and Williamina McKinnon and their surviving three children, James, Benjamin and Gilbert George, returned to Watten in Caithness.

John McKinnon died 7 March 1943 at the Shielton farm where he had been born. Williamina lived on for another 20 years, dying on 24 September 1963 at Ackergill, near Wick.

Casualty of War

By the time of the First World War most of the Caithness men who had gone to Patagonia were resident in Argentina or Chile, so they were not actively involved in the war. Many of them did, however, support relief funds such as the Widows and Orphans Fund and the Patriotic Fund. David Bain, the youngest of the Bain brothers and still in Scotland, had enlisted in the Seaforth Highlanders in 1911 and was in the 7th Company, 5th Battalion Seaforth Highlanders during the war. He emigrated to Patagonia after the war was over. Another Caithness Patagonian Pioneer did, however, suffer the ultimate fate of wartime; George and William Hendry having arrived back in Britain in 1915, George was killed in action in France in 1918.

Four Hendry brothers from the Clyth/Lybster area in Caithness were among the Caithness Patagonian contingent. At various times, John, George, James and William lived and worked in Patagonia. Their parents were James Hendry, born 1854 and Jessie (Jane) (née Bain), born 3 September 1858. Their mother's family was related to the Bain family from Mavesy. In fact the Hendry family lived near the Bains, in the Mavesy area between Lybster and Clyth.

John Hendry, the eldest of the brothers, was born 1 November 1883 at Mavesy. He departed for Patagonia some time after 1901. We know that he was in Rio Zurdo from 1914 at least through to 1917. He became a sheep manager, and he married Janet MacIntosh in Patagonia on 31 March 1912; in 1920 he brought her and their young family – Alex Tillie aged 5, John George aged 4, and Donald William aged 4 months – to Scotland. John died on 22 May 1945 and is buried in Rio Gallegos.

George Hendry was born on 21 October 1888 at Mavesy. In 1906, along with his neighbour, George Bain, he set sail from Liverpool for Punta Arenas on 16 August. George Hendry made a brief return trip to Scotland in 1912, this time with his brother James. The two then returned to Patagonia, sailing from Liverpool to Punta Arenas on 17 September 1912. Sinclair Sutherland, another Clyth man, also went to Patagonia with them.

George returned to Scotland again on 31 May 1915, this time with his brother William; the aim was to enlist in the First World War forces. George served as a sergeant in the 13th Battalion (Scottish Horse) Black Watch, but was killed in action in France on 4 November 1918.

William Bain Hendry was born on 19 June 1890 at Mavesy, and by 1914 he was in Patagonia. William, like many others, as a way of supporting the war effort

138

donated to the Widows and Orphans Fund run by the *Magellan Times* newspaper. At that time he was employed at Estancia Rincon los Morros, which was located near the Chilean–Argentine border. This estancia extended over nine miles and was, by Patagonian standards, one of the most modern in terms of equipment; the shearing shed had eight hydraulic press scissors, and the estancia employed 20 labourers. William returned to Britain, along with his brother George, to enlist in the First World War. After the war, in 1919, he returned to Patagonia. Some time later, he decided to return to Caithness, but legend has it that he found it difficult to settle; so he set off once again to Patagonia. He departed from Caithness on 8 December 1933. He died in Patagonia on 14 March 1975 and is buried in Rio Gallegas.

James Hendry was the fourth of the brothers to go to Patagonia. He was born at Parkside, Lybster, on 25 October 1894, and in 1911 he was employed as a cattleman at Plantation Farm, Lybster. He departed for Patagonia with his brother George on 17 September 1912, and in 1914 was living with his other brother, John, at Rio Zurdo. James arrived back in Liverpool on 5 January 1921; potentially he came home for his sister's marriage – Sinclair Hendry was to marry Donald Miller Dunnet on 15 April 1921. James may have remained in Scotland afterwards.

The brothers' father, James Hendry senior, died on 2 November 1922. He was another of the many Caithness patients being treated at Sunnyside Hospital in Montrose. His wife Jessie (Jane) appears to have lived with her daughter, Sinclair Dunnet, near Glasgow, and lived on until 8 December 1940.

Leaving Clyth

The Clyth area of Caithness provided Patagonia with a number of pioneers. The Nicolson brothers, Robert and Donald, and their nephew Alexander were all Clyth born and bred. The Bains were close by at Mavesy, and their neighbours were the Hendry brothers – all to become Patagonians. James Plowman, although born in Wick, lived some of his early years at East Clyth. Sinclair and John Sutherland, another two Patagonian Pioneer brothers, lived at Occumster. One of the earliest to leave for Patagonia was John MacLeod, whose family was resident at Mid Clyth.

The Clyth Estate, on which these families were tenants, belonged to a Mr Sharp. He is remembered as one of the landlord class in Scotland who was blamed for unfair rent increases. The people of Clyth protested at the proposed increases, but perhaps the potential of a new life in Patagonia was more appealing to them than scraping a living from the Caithness soil and sea.

John Macleod was born c. 1853. His father was Donald MacLeod and his mother was Elizabeth (Lizzie) (née Gunn). John had a number of brothers and sisters who in 1861 were all resident at Mid Clyth. He probably left for Patagonia in the early 1890s with his neighbour, William Bain. It is thought that they sailed initially for the Falkland Islands and while William moved on to Patagonia, John may have remained in the Falklands for a few years. His movements in Patagonia are somewhat sketchy but he apparently settled in Bahia Laura. Legend has it that his house was assembled from a series of wooden sections he had shipped from Britain. Given the scarcity of building materials in the region, this may well have made economic sense.

John was married twice. His first wife was Mary Baumer, with whom he had three children, Ellen, Alice Mary and Donald John Alexander. Something either happened to or was of concern to John in 1900, because on 3 May 1900 he recorded a will at Punta Arenas; maybe he was about to embark on a long journey or perhaps he became unwell. Given that he lived until 1930, the latter seems less likely.

By the time the will was made, John's first wife was deceased. His second wife was Margaret Lizzie (née MacGregor) and by 1900 they had three children, so the will could well have been about accommodating his two families: his daughter Jessie had been born at Cape Negro near Punta Arenas on 9 January 1895; on 12 November 1897 a son, John George, had also been born at Cape Negro; and a daughter, Margaret Lizzie, is also listed in the will. A further child, Robertina Alexina, was born around 1909.

John's mother, Elizabeth (née Gunn) died at Mid Clyth on 5 June 1901, while his father Donald lived on until 1912, by which time he would have been nearing 90 years of age.

John brought his family to Caithness in 1914. They arrived at Liverpool from Punta Arenas on 21 June 1914. A fellow passenger was another Caithness Patagonian shepherd, James Earsman.

John died on 22 March 1930 and is buried in Puerto Deseado. His son John George, who died on 8 February 1938, is also buried in Puerto Deseado.

A Dunbeath Family Leaves for Patagonia

Work was not always easy to come by in late 19th-century Caithness. The fishing industry was past its peak and the many men who had learned trades such as masonry and carpentry were forced to look for work elsewhere. Some of those who left for the sheep farming in Patagonia were Caithness joiners; while they put these skills to good use in the development of the Patagonian estancias, it was as shepherds they were employed. Others from Caithness found work in cities such as Edinburgh.

Benjamin Gunn Cormack was born on 3 May 1892 in Edinburgh. His parents, David Cormack and Jessie (née Gunn), originally from Caithness, lived at Lauriston Place, Edinburgh, where David worked as a house painter. The two had married in Edinburgh on 23 July 1891. David had been born at Dunbeath in 1854 and Jessie Gunn in 1856, also in Dunbeath.

At the time of his marriage to Jessie, David was a widower with an existing family in Edinburgh, so maybe it was no great surprise that by the time of the 1901 census Ben, child of David's second wife, had moved away from Edinburgh to Caithness, where he lived with his uncle Allan Gunn, at Badnagie, Dunbeath. Ben continued living there during 1911, working as a shepherd. Allan Gunn remained at Badnagie, working as a crofter and fisherman until his death on 3 April 1935.

On 8 December 1911 Ben married Lucy Gair Jane Miller.

Lucy Gair Jane Miller was born 19 April 1891 at Knockinnon, Dunbeath, daughter of John Miller, crofter and fisherman, and his wife Christina (née Mowat). Christina died on 8 July 1900, leaving nine-year-old Lucy in the care of her father and his own mother Jane Miller, and an aunt, Lucy G. Miller. There was also a younger brother, James M. Miller.

Unlike many of those who left Caithness for Patagonia, Ben and Lucy Cormack had established themselves as a family before emigrating. A son, John Millar, was born to them at Badnagie on 16 March 1912, followed by their second son, Benjamin Gunn, born at the Miller home in Knockinnon, Dunbeath, on 29 May 1913. Around this time the decision to depart for Patagonia was taken, and Ben sailed from Liverpool to Punta Arenas on 19 July 1913. Lucy and the two boys followed on 8 July 1916. A daughter, Jessie Cristina, was born in Patagonia on 31 October 1918, and in 1921 the family was completed with the birth of Alan Gunn.

Ben junior died on 25 May 1941, aged only 27; Ben senior died on 24 November 1968 and is buried in Punta Arenas.

Off to Patagonia Again

The Caithness Patagonians who made their homes in Argentina would make return trips home – some regularly. There were also those who never saw Caithness again, whether by choice or circumstance; and there were some who did not settle in Patagonia and returned to their native hearth. John Cormack Mowat was, however, almost unique amongst the Caithness Patagonians in that he returned home after a few years, but after a further five years set off to the south again. Seven years later he was back in Scotland again, this time for good.

John Cormack Mowat was born on 13 July 1869 at Olrig, the son of James Mowat, a gardener, and Isabella (née Mackenzie). James had been born in 1831, also in Olrig. Isabella had come from Canisbay and had been born there in 1835. James and Isabella had married in Canisbay on 8 July 1864; James was working as an agricultural labourer and living at Netherside House, Olrig; Isabella was a domestic servant at Olrig House. Prior to John's birth, two daughters, Christina and Margaret, were born, in 1866 and 1868 respectively, and by 1871 the family were resident in Kirkhouse Kitchen, Olrig. Another son, William George, died shortly after his birth in 1874, and Christina died from the measles at the age of 17 in 1883. Three years later, John's mother died, on 9 July 1886. The 1891 census records only James and his daughter Margaret at Kirkhouse, Olrig; at this time, his son John was working as a farm servant at Harpsdale, Halkirk.

Shortly afterwards John appeared in Patagonian records; in the 1895 Argentine census he is listed as a farmhand near Rio Gallegas. He must have made a trip home in or around 1898, as he departed Liverpool for Punta Arenas on 6 October 1898. In 1900 he was back in Caithness, arriving in Liverpool on 19 April. He again took up residence with his father James and sister Margaret at Olrig, now resident at the Porter's Lodge.

James died on 29 November 1904 at The Lodge, Olrig House, and within a year of his death, John was off again to Patagonia. On 14 September 1905 he and two other Caithness Patagonians, Henry Christian and Sinclair Bremner, departed Liverpool for Punta Arenas.

Patagonia was not, however, destined to be John Mowat's home, as he returned to Caithness again on 16 November 1912. Some time later he settled in Glasgow and was employed there as a chemical worker. He remained unmarried, and died in that city on 10 January 1932. His sister Margaret signed his death certificate, and John is buried in Cathcart Cemetery.

To Patagonia and Beyond

Many of the Caithness Patagonian Pioneers crossed the Atlantic Ocean on more than one occasion. Return trips home or simply coming home for good were the most common reasons for undertaking the journeys, but some of these men travelled further around the world: Percy Earsman, in his latter Patagonian years, went on a trip to Adelaide, in Australia; Angus McPherson left Patagonia and settled for a period in Canada, before returning to Patagonia; of the two Sutherland brothers, Sinclair left Patagonia and settled back in Caithness but John Hymers moved on from Patagonia to a life in New Zealand.

Sinclair Sutherland was born on 10 May 1895 at West Clyth in Caithness. His brother, **John Hymers Sutherland**, was born 26 May 1897 at Mavesy, Lybster. Their parents were Robert Sutherland and Mary (née Hymers). Robert Sutherland had been born in 1864 in Latheron Parish, and Mary had been born 15 October 1865 at Lochs on the Hebridean island of Lewis. Mary's father, John Hymers, was a sheep farm manager at Lochs, one of the more controversial sheep runs of the period, but by the time of the 1881 census the Hymers family had moved to a farm at Clyth, where John now farmed 100 acres of arable land.

Robert Sutherland and Mary Hymers had married on 2 December 1892 at Clyth; Robert was a fisherman and Mary worked as a domestic servant in West Clyth. The family had established their home at Occumster, where in 1900 a daughter, Mary J., was born. There were four further additions to the family: Susanna born 13 February 1902; Jessie Hymers born 3 July 1904; William born 1907; and in 1909, Robertina. On 21 November 1910, their father Robert died at the relatively young age of 46.

In 1911, the two brothers, Sinclair and John, were still resident in Caithness; John remained at home in Mavesy, while Sinclair worked as a ploughman at Kensary, near Watten. The following year however, Sinclair left for Patagonia; along with his neighbours George and James Hendry, he departed on 17 September 1912.

By 1914 Sinclair was in the Puerto Deseado area of Santa Cruz province. John followed his brother in 1920, sailing from Southampton to Buenos Aires on 24 September 1920. Sinclair began a series of trips between Patagonia and Caithness in 1921 or 1922; he is recorded as departing for Buenos Aires on 10 February 1922. But in 1930 he was back in Caithness again – and off to Patagonia once more on 20 February 1931. It has been claimed that his intention was to permanently return home, but as his friends were all gone he simply headed back to Patagonia. He did however finally return to Caithness, and died at Hillhead, Lybster, on 2 January 1962.

John left Patagonia in March 1925 and, following a brief stopover in Britain, continued his travels, to make a new life for himself in New Zealand; he departed Southampton for Wellington in New Zealand on 17 July 1925, and in 1928 he married Rosie Marti.

On the Fringes

Caithness was by no means the only area of Scotland that supplied people to open up the Patagonian sheep farming industry. The Western Isles, in particular Lewis, developed a strong Patagonian connection, which has been expertly documented by Greta MacKenzie.[1] A Lewis man, Angus Shaw, married Jessie Bain; and her sister, Rebecca, married Lachlan MacDonald from Tiree. Caithness' neighbouring county, Sutherland, also has associations. Alexander Sutherland, originally from Brora, was a well-known and respected Patagonian shepherd, and one of his daughters, Margaret, married Caithness Patagonian Percy Earsman.

The area of Strath Halladale sits astride the Caithness–Sutherland county boundary. The family of the two Patagonian Pioneers **Alexander and Robert MacDonald** retain strong links with the area. Their father, Robert MacDonald, had been born at Dalhalvaig, Halladale, in the Parish of Reay in Caithness, and their mother Esther (née Curry Tully) had been born in neighbouring Kildonan. Robert and Esther had married on 20 May 1859 at Loth.

Robert senior was a shepherd and it was often the case that the shepherd's family would move from area to area. In 1871 the Macdonald family resided at Creich in Sutherland.

Alexander was born in 1861, then Robert junior was born 25 February 1872; by the time of the 1881 census, the family lived at Achany, near Lairg in Sutherland. Alexander now worked as a shepherd and Robert was a scholar.

The precise date when Alexander first left for Patagonia is uncertain, but Robert is believed to have arrived there around 1888, when he was initially employed as a shepherd on one of John Hamilton's sheep farms. Alexander returned to Scotland by 1894, when he married Barbara McPherson from Tain, on 20 December 1894. Alexander and his new wife sailed for Punta Arenas on 16 February 1895.

In 1895 Robert was employed as a manager at Estancia Ruben Aike, near Rio Gallegas. The following year he married Spanish-born Fernanda Garcia. By 1900 the MacDonald family, which included three-year old son Robert Francis, had become established in their own estancia, called La Vanguardia. The family grew, with Walter born in 1903, William born 1905, Laura Elizabeth born 1907 and Mabel Olive born 1909. Robert and his family made a trip to Britain in 1912, arriving in London from La Plata on 8 June 1912. On the return journey they departed on 3 October 1912, sailing this time from Liverpool to Punta Arenas.

The next trip home, however, proved fatal for Robert; while travelling between Buenos Aires and London he died on board the *Rosia*, on 4 July 1920. His wife Fernanda and the family finally arrived in London on 26 July 1920. Fernanda and the family returned to Patagonia on 21 October 1920, and she took over the reins of the MacDonald Patagonian farms, managing and developing the business. She and her children made two return trips to Britain during 1925; the address she provided in Scotland was 50 Union Road, Inverness.

Alexander, meanwhile, had returned home and bought Novar Farm before settling in Inverness. He died at 57 Old Edinburgh Road, Inverness, on 18 September 1942.

---

1 *Return to Patagonia/* Greta Mackenzie. Islands Book Trust 2011.

The Electrician

The reasons why people left Caithness for Patagonia are now often clouded in the mists of time. The parents, brothers and sisters of those who went to Patagonia are all now gone, and many of their memories have gone with them. Some of the current generation have gathered letters, photos and artefacts in a bid to capture something of their Patagonian ancestors, but others do not know why their ancestors made the epic journey. John Harper's daughter Margaret, when asked in an interview at her Patagonian home in the early 2000s why her father had moved there, did not know; it had never been specifically talked about. Nevertheless, Margaret was aware of her Scottish origins – her brother John was always known as Jock, and she was quite clear that her father had originally come from Wick.

John Harper was born on 4 June 1883 at Tolbooth Lane, Wick. His father, William Harper was a master shoemaker in Wick and his mother was Maggie Janet (Jane) (née Dallas). Maggie came from Edinburgh, and her marriage took place in the city on 5 November 1874.

At the time of the 1881 census, the Harper family lived in Willowbank, Wick, and William Harper employed four men in his shoemaking business. By 1891 the family had moved to 28 Moray Street in Wick. John Harper, aged seven, was a scholar, possibly attending the nearby West Banks School. In 1895, William Harper's shoemaker's shop was located in the High Street in Wick.

John Harper departed for Patagonia in 1907, sailing from Liverpool to Punta Arenas – but unlike most of his fellow Caithness Patagonians, he did not follow the shepherding trade. Instead, he found work as an electrician for the Punta Arenas Electric Light Company.

William's brother, James Dallas Harper, also left home in Wick, setting up as a grocer in Inverness. In 1911 he married Jane MacMillan, the daughter of a Glasgow hotel proprietor. James then moved into the hotel business, and in 1915 was a hotel proprietor in Lybster. He then signed up for active service during the First World War, only to be killed in France on 31 July 1918.

In 1912 John married Ada Kirwin, the daughter of a contract employee of the Falklands Island Company. She had been born on 5 September 1874 in Liverpool. Before she met John, she had worked in Rio Gallegos as a nursemaid.

Their first child, also named John, was born on 31 November 1912. A second son, Arthur Dallas, followed in 1914, and a daughter, Margaret, on 23 July 1915.

Margaret became a teacher at the British School in Punta Arenas, and in her latter years was often consulted by visitors on the history of the town.

The eldest son, John (known in Patagonia as Jock), married Jane Eva Essex Carter, the daughter of Rowland William Essex Carter, a New Zealander. Rowland was an agricultural officer and stock inspector employed by the New Zealand government, and he worked with the Falkland Islands Government. Jane's mother was Anna (or Ada) Otzen, born in Germany. She had emigrated to Punta Arenas c. 1910. John and Jane Harper's family consisted of Juan Arturo, born 1952 in Buenos Aires, David born 1955 and Jacqueline Anne born 1962 in Punta Arenas.

John and Ada's second son, Arthur Dallas, married Virginia Rose Tetzlaff on 22 February 1941.

John died on 26 April 1936 in Punta Arenas, and he is buried there in the Municipal Cemetery, alongside his family: Ada, who died on 22 August 1957; John (Jock), who died on 10 March 1993; and his sister Margaret, who died on 27 August 2005. John's mother, Maggie Jane (née Dallas) Harper, had died in Glasgow on 3 August 1941.

The Gamekeeper

The Scottish moors and rivers were deliberately earmarked as a hunting playground for the rich and the landed. The role of the gamekeeper in Scotland is one of preservation and supply; he must ensure that stocks are at sufficient levels to give the hunters and fishermen a reasonable chance of success. The gamekeeper is also something of a law-enforcing policeman; since the game birds, animals and fish are on private property he is charged with keeping poachers at bay. In Patagonia it was the guanaco that was the beast most hunted; it was an important source of food and clothing for the indigenous population of Patagonia. The early Patagonian Pioneers and shepherds were quick to follow the native tradition of killing guanaco, and as a result, today guanaco are considerably reduced from their original numbers. No gamekeepers were in evidence then – Patagonia's game was a free-for-all.

William Sutherland Ross grew up as the son of a gamekeeper in Caithness. While not a great deal is known about his time in Patagonia, his hunting skills must surely have been useful.

William Sutherland Ross was born on 6 December 1896 at Strathmore. He was the third child of Andrew Ross and Christina Sutherland: a brother, Adam born 11 June 1892, and a sister, Margaret born in 1895, had preceded him. Andrew had come from a long line of gamekeepers, and his own father, Adam Ross, had been a gamekeeper at Glencorse, near Edinburgh. By the census of 1881, Adam and family were at Strathmore, where he was again employed as gamekeeper. In 1901, William's father, Andrew, had been assistant gamekeeper at Strathmore, but in 1911 the family had moved to Ben Morven Distillery Cottages, Halkirk, Andrew still being employed as a gamekeeper. This family association with the land continued. William's brother, Adam, was employed as a gardener at Gerston at the time of his marriage to Elizabeth MacAdie MacDonald in 1921.

In 1923, William joined the Caithness Patagonian community. He sailed from Liverpool to Punta Arenas on 6 September 1923; on the same ship was Percy Earsman, making a return trip to Patagonia.

We know little of William's time in Patagonia. His destination address on departure in 1923 was Punta Arenas in Patagonia, but when he returned to Caithness on 20 June 1931, the passenger list shows his last place of residence as the Falkland Islands.

William Sutherland Ross died in Halkirk on 25 July 1980.

The Sheep Dealer

The Caithness Patagonian Pioneers, not surprisingly, became expert in the business of sheep and sheep farming. John McGregor, who grew up at Westerseat Farm, Wick, was to become a Patagonian sheep dealer.

John McGregor was born on 25 September 1886 at Springpark, Thurso, son of William McGregor and Betsy (née Anderson Ferrier). William was a locomotive engine driver, and had been born in Inverness on 15 January 1848. Betsy had come from significant Orkney farming stock. She had been born 20 March 1858 at Hobbister Farm, Orphir, in Orkney. By 1871 the Ferrier family were farming at Springpark in Thurso, by 1891 they were on the farm of Westerseat, Wick, and by 1911 they were at the farm of Ackergill Mains.

In 1901, John, along with his mother, sister Annie and brothers Robert and Donald, were resident at Westerseat Farm. By 1908, John had made his way to Patagonia. His time in Patagonia remains unknown, but by 1921 he was sailing from Liverpool to Punta Arenas with his profession recorded as sheep buyer. His address was Westerseat Farm, so whether he had simply been home to visit or on sheep buying duty is unclear. Was he buying sheep from Caithness for Patagonia? Or had he concluded a deal that would bring Patagonian sheep to Caithness?

Who Was He?

Tracking down the Caithness Patagonians has been fun and at times a challenge. The discovery of their lives and experiences in Patagonia has owed much to their descendants in Argentina and Caithness. Gathering information about their families and places in Caithness has often been the easier task, given the considerable amount of public access data that exists in Scotland – except, that is, for the records of Sinclair Bremner, whose trips to and from Patagonia, and some details of his Patagonian life, have been readily available. The Caithness side of his story, however, is something of a mystery. Exactly who he was remains a conundrum. The basic problem is that three individuals with the name of Sinclair Bremner were born in Caithness at almost the exact same date.

Will the real Sinclair Bremner please reveal himself?

Sinclair Bremner was born in Caithness in c. 1886. In the 1891 census there was a Sinclair Bremner aged 5, living in Canisbay with his parents Sinclair and Mary Bremner; Sinclair senior was a crofter. There was also a Sinclair Bremner aged 5, living at 66 Kinnaird Street, Wick, with his parents, George and Dolina Bremner; George was a cooper. Thirdly, there was a Sinclair Cooper Bremner, again aged 5, living at 14 Union Street, Wick, with his parents John and Edith Bremner, John Bremner being employed as a clerk.

Whichever Sinclair Bremner it was that had departed for Patagonia on 14 September 1905, accompanied by two others from Caithness – Henry Christian and John Mowat – he arrived back in Britain on 1 May 1912, again with Henry Christian.

In 1914 a Sinclair Bremner (the same individual? Or perhaps another of the three Sinclairs?) is recorded as leasing some 10,000 hectares of land in Patagonia. He married Eveline Augusta Hepworth on 12 December 1919, in Punta Arenas. How the two had got to know each other is also a mystery; Eveline Augusta Hepworth had departed Liverpool for Punta Arenas on 6 November 1919, a month before the marriage took place. Two years later Mr and Mrs Sinclair Bremner set sail from Buenos Aires, firstly for Southampton, then onwards from Southampton to Wellington, New Zealand.